For My Mother,
Margaret.

TABLE OF CONTENTS

INTRODUCTION

Introduction

Our world is changing. She is awakening and we follow in her footsteps...

I believe we all have the power to choose what happens next and that the path to global renaissance is through a wave of personal internal revolutions. We have the ability to make the future all that we desire it to be. Veils of illusion that have been apart of this grand experiment for eons are in the process of being ripped away. The quest for truth is on the rise, and through that process, we are growing expediently. We are coming to terms with our shadow and the shadow of this world. We are waking up. This book is a collection of ideologies, practices, and stories aimed at initiating you onto the path of alchemizing your energetic and emotional space. It will introduce you to aspects of the spiritual world and provide you with ways to initiate contact with your divine self.

Mysteries are resurrecting themselves, mysteries that many have tried to suppress from our legacy. To change the state of the earth we must choose to explore and resurrect the essence of our own souls. This is a global transmutation, but for the seeker, it will begin by venturing into the realms of solitude and reflection. We can get as frustrated as we want, but it will not feed what we require to make us great. We can give up and let it all burn, or we can overcome. We can create something new.

Growing up, this world made little sense to me. In my bones I knew there was something wrong, so much pain, it all seemed avoidable. If there were a God, or a Goddess, or ANYONE out there, why is it that so many of us suffer? Why would they create beings to be beautiful and yet so cruel? Why is life different for all of us, and how is it that some cope so easily? I was angry, and frankly, I didn't want to be alive. There was a pervading darkness like a shroud of anxiety hanging over me. No matter how hard I tried, I couldn't escape it and could not authentically connect or open up to anyone. I learned very quickly how to hide who I was, how to escape reality, how to tell people what they wanted to hear, and check out of this world—anything to dull the pain.

Plagued from an early age by suicidal thoughts and urges, I felt alone, as though I didn't fit in, and longed for something I couldn't quite recall. It was a sadness I didn't understand, hearing voices and not knowing where they were coming from. Least to say, it was sort of a dreary time. Now I know that I chose a path of accelerated growth, because I wanted to learn. My choice to accumulate pain and shadow was because I am an alchemist, knowing one day I would heal, and all I gathered would be used as the energetic fuel to power the fire of my dreams. I just had to change the darkness, and let it go.

We are ascending, coming into a new wave of power. We have

waited for this since long forgotten lands sunk into the sea, launching us on a journey of density and redemption, rebuilding and re-birthing, waiting for the light to return and rule again. We are being given the opportunity to change our ways, to walk into a new earth, a new dimension of living. Now, if we choose it, we can return home.

Home as in the womb of unconditional love, living from the spark of the divine energy in your heart. Living for love, from the soul, that is what will change the world. Active, deep, complex, vivid love, for that is what and who we truly are. We're in the middle of a cosmic storm leading us to a myriad of new beginnings. Stay in the eye, find your center. Wherever you are in the world, whatever your battles may be, however you're feeling in this moment: Stay strong. Find the light and follow it. Do what you love and let nothing stand in your way, and if one sentence in this book helps one person with that, then I have succeeded in my intent.

This, all coming from a girl who spent her 19th birthday in jail for the possession and consumption of illegal narcotics. I can remember them pulling me from my mother's arms. She had followed me that night, trying to convince me to come home. I remember her face, her tears, her screams, and my own, as the officers pulled us apart. To the law I was a criminal. To her, I was her little girl, and to myself? To myself I was lost, wishing myself a happy birthday face down on a concrete slab in a plastic encased room, wondering how in the hell I got there. I was filled with self hatred and had no ability to traverse or release it on my own. Laying there in that filthy bunk, hoping the bologna they fed us was fit for human consumption, I prayed. I prayed to something I didn't believe existed, and I asked for help. Deciding no matter what happened, I would never be where I was again. I committed myself to change. I don't regret these moments and am grateful for every lesson, because it led me to where I am today: writing a book that will hopefully help someone like the girl I once was. This book is in memory of her because she had to perish, for the woman I am now to be born.

So if you are in a place where you are scared or even suicidal hold on, know that you aren't alone, that you are a warrior and you came to this world with great purpose. Don't let your pain beat you. Keep breathing, keep learning. My story is not a sad one. It is one of a seeker, a creator, an alchemist, and I could not be more appreciative for this life and the path I have walked to manifest this experience. I want to share where I came from so you can see the polarities between where I started and where I am now: a successful career doing what I enjoy, at peace, married to the man I love, satisfied with myself and my experience. I have true and valued friends and am deeply connected to my family. I have been taken on a journey and shown the divine forces that inhabit our world and what they can do, if we allow them to do it, having myself been guided by Spirit from darkness into light and changed wholeheartedly by that process.

To Spirit and all who have helped me along my path, to those who knocked me down, because they showed me nothing could keep me there for long, and to that younger self who never let her light be extinguished—I am grateful, overcome with joy, and this is truly a miraculous thing.

WHAT IS AN ALCHEMIST?

Alchemy has existed since the dawn of time, its influence rippling through our history in many different directions. She is the wise grandmother of modern chemistry, medicine, scientific pursuit, and her meaning has been hotly debated throughout her legacy. Historically, alchemy is said to be the process of attempting to turn base metals into gold; however, our recorded history is skim at best. The alchemical arts were passed down orally from master to student for thousands of years, so our written history is limited and has many symbols that have been left to interpretation. This was done intentionally, so as to guard the secrets of the Mysteries, which so many sought to stomp out or exploit for nefarious gain.

There are many languages to alchemy, but to me, alchemy is about transformation and transmutation of the self and of the world, using the subtle powers that govern and move this universe. The history of our true abilities as energetic beings and creators was forgotten and is on the rise again. To find the truth, we must voyage inside ourselves to rekindle the ancient knowledge which has been lost for generations. Walking this path is an intention to seek truth and awareness in all you are and all you do. You are asking to serve your calling and your light beyond the pleasures and pay offs of the small self. It is not always easy to look into your darkness and see its true nature. You are looking not only at your own shadow, but at the world's, for they reflect each other, and only that which is uncovered is able to be transmuted.

An alchemist is an initiate in the mysteries of life, a voyager of the infinite, dedicated to the path of creation, seeking to master the self so that they may find the salvation underneath. Through focus and the process of reincarnation, we work at discovering the gold that is hidden within us. "Gold" that is available to us when we stand in our divine knowledge and power underneath our various layers of earthly density. An alchemist is someone who has answered the call of the unseen realms, who seeks to align with their most profound intention, and reveal the secrets that make up the process of creation.

We are all alchemists. Maybe not in the most traditional sense, but we are all given lives and energy to mold into our greatest intention, though we may not remember this on a conscious level. There may be much dis-ease and unrest in our realm but that is not new. What IS new is the collective response to it. We are rising up as a united force to that which has kept this earth in bondage, in so, becoming more aware, and more compassionate. We are opening our hearts whilst simultaneously revealing the shadow that has circulated through this world since the dawn of its descension. It can be confusing, but chaos is apart of the process of creation.

I seek to bring the ideas of alchemy into everyday life. You can alchemize your emotions, your reality and yourself. You can harness the power of the unseen forces, the power of your spirit, to change and transform your experience and from that process you will change the world. For when one of us heals, we all heal. Just as if one of hurts, we all suffer. The basic principles covered in the following chapters make up the introductory foundation to your relationship with the unseen realms, the healing of your spirit, and education in the alchemical arts. I write for the aspiring alchemist. You are a sleeper cell filled with ancient knowledge, that if recalled will contribute to this world rising again. May you walk in love and light on your path to greatness.

SPARK:
A GUIDE FOR THE ASPIRING ALCHEMIST

CREATED BY BARBARA ESTELLE DEJESUS
ILLUSTRATED BY GAETANO CARLUCCI

WHAT ARE WE DOING HERE?

We all come from one base energy. I refer to this energy as "All That Is," "God/Goddess," "Source Energy," or simply "Spirit," though I don't think it matters what you call it. It is the essence of pure unconditional love, that is the basis of all creation. This energy is Masculine and Feminine, both equally important to the whole.

There was a time when magic was an integral part of many of earth's tribes and societies, where energy and the knowledge to navigate it was well known. Throughout our legacy on this planet magic has been attacked, forced into hiding or destroyed. In the present, it is reemerging once again as people are waking up to its truth. Quantum Physicists are only now discovering what spiritualists have claimed since the beginning, that we are all connected and come from a unified energetic source. The world of Spirit is not separate from our physical world, it exists within and all around us. For clarification, when I say "Spirit" I am referring to Source Energy or All That Is, as opposed to "spirit," your personal spirit. You have a physical flesh and bone body, but this is only a vessel for your spirit. The third dimensional physical world with which you are familiar is only one layer of the energetic anatomy.

"You" are a universe of energetic activity. A being of light that has come from some fantastic part of the galaxy to lend your power to the mission we are all on. This physical reality is a reflection of the Spirit world. The state of your spirit and spiritual body will be reflected in your physical experience. All pain and dis-ease are first manifest on an energetic rather than physical level, meaning the more you align yourself with your spirit and work on your energetic anatomy, the more powerful and enchanting your life will become.

I believe our cosmic journey began in the essence of curiosity. I think there was a bright light, a source of consciousness and that consciousness had an idea. It wanted to learn so it decided to do so, shooting itself in every direction of the galaxy, beginning a cycle of cosmic creation. We are pieces of that Source, of the divine creative consciousness. Thus, we are creators and explorers. The soul comes to earth to mature, to experience, to evolve. Earth is a school where you learn how to manipulate and navigate energy. We do not remember this when we arrive, so now many of us feel isolated, depressed or a myriad of other sordid emotions. Your spirit cries out to feel connected again, though in fact, there was never really a separation.

The physical world is not our home, it is a simulation we created. As Shakespeare said "All the world's a stage, and all the men and women merely players." It is a grand play, an experiment. This experiment is not for the weak, if you come here, you know that you are being born into a world that experiences confusion and widespread suffering, that you will bare the heavy weight of earthly attachments, and be tested on every level. It is a realm for those who wish to learn quickly. Our energetic evolution is infinite. We, as one body of cosmic consciousness, will never cease to move through the galaxies creating worlds and legacies. It is on a constantly shifting continuum furthering the intention to balance and grow itself. We are currently undergoing a massive awakening. Mother Earth rises again and is guiding us into her warm embrace, but not before she turns the world upside down and regains balance across her plains. This cycle is tumultuous as the veils of illusion that have covered the truth of this world are rapidly being lifted away and we are witnessing the seedy underbelly of our collective shadow.

This world is not owned by corporations, politicians, governments or humanity's societal structures. Throughout the history of the light and dark forces attempting to balance themselves on earth, many have tried to manipulate, overtake, or exploit her but she cannot be owned for she is an entity in herself, birthing us and holding space for our evolution. These dark forces are now being siphoned out, and their energy is expiring as this awakening progresses (even when it doesn't seem like that on the surface). This is why our current political climate can seem so bleak at times, because we are being called to take our power back from these systems, remembering that we are sovereign creative beings, capable of shifting and changing this world into anything we like.

We are here to choose a new kind of earth. The masters inhabit our world at this time, the prophets, the saviors, the poets and the artists. We are them. The same souls that walked this path before, and before. You are a master in creation, in manifestation, in magic and the power of thought or you would not be here at this time. We have the opportunity to remember who we are, the power of our souls, and to use that power to create something beautiful. Your purpose is in your presence. Simply in your being here, your light is in service to this new blueprint. There is a great power being reintegrated into our collective, and like a surfer in the ocean, the better we learn to ride the waves, the better the view going through.

We are in the midst of a revolution. If we arm ourselves with the strength of our divinity, we will soar higher than we have ever before, but it is our decision. Free will is sacred to Spirit and will always be respected. When we plug into our Source, call upon our spirit and the vast light army it consists of, everything is possible, and that is why we are here. To contribute our light to the auspicious happenings of our time, creating a new way of living on this planet, following the call of roads less traveled, and fostering a world of inclusion and harmony.

Say the following invocation in support of the shift we are experiencing in our collective at this time. The more of us who believe and lend our power to supporting the new world that is being birthed, the swifter, smoother and all together better our collective manifestation will be. You are powerful. The earth is so grateful for all who are calling upon more light and grounding it within her, so she may birth us all into a new existence.

New World Invocation:

I awaken my authentic self, and activate my role in this auspicious new beginning for Mother Earth. I am strong, and I have purpose. I am meant to be here, and I am mentally, spiritually and emotionally free. I welcome and invoke a world of inclusion, harmony, unconditional love and ask to be the best I can be in support of that mission. I recognize and affirm my divine heritage and ask that the world be flooded with celestial light, love, and assistance during this historical and palpable energetic shift.

By my own free will, in gratitude, and so it is.

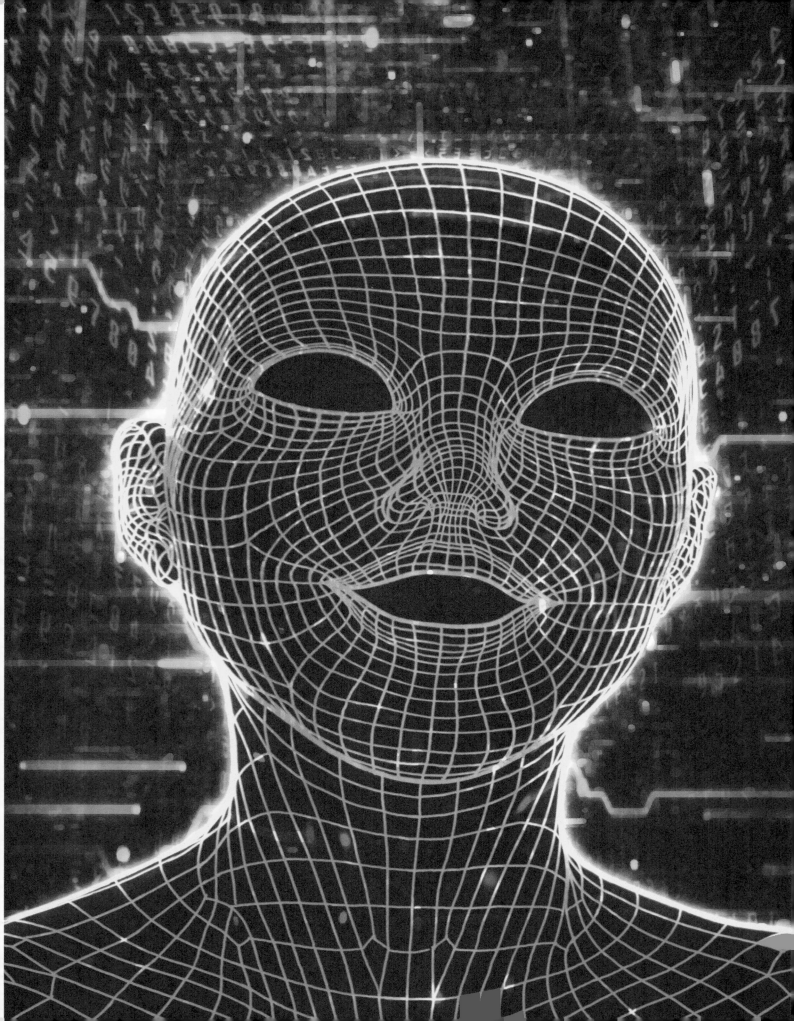

THIS IS A MATRIX

We live in a Matrix. A simulation where we are given the opportunity to assume a flesh and bone physical body and learn how to navigate the 3rd dimensional experience. It's an ancient cosmic game that we designed around ourselves to help us learn and elevate to the next levels of our journey. This Matrix is governed by certain laws. One of them being the law of free will. Having free will basically means that we are allowed to do, think or say anything and everything we wish. We have the power to choose our actions and reactions which are in response to the physical universe we have inserted ourselves into. This does not mean that consequences do not exist for there are also laws like the law of attraction and karma, but we are free to choose our paths as we go, even when it doesn't seem that way.

Though pop culture references to the Matrix are entertaining, I believe the mechanics are much more complex than they have been portrayed in movies and sci-fi programs. The technology behind it is far more advanced than anything our scientific community has executed thus far. We are not being held against our will, we have volunteered for a virtual reality game and when we arrive all memory of who we are is blocked until we are ready to awaken. We have had many other civilizations on this planet that were in sync and understanding of the way reality was created around them, but the histories of those societies have been hidden and not much record of them exists. Though, more pieces of the story will continue to wash ashore as the years go by and this awakening progresses.

Understanding the nature of the world in which you live can assist you to create the life you desire, to discover where you came from, and where you are meant to go. You create the world around you with your thoughts, feelings, intentions, emotions and actions. When you learn the rules of the game, you can change it. When you master the game, you can win it. What's winning? A life of love, joy and satiation of the soul. By achieving that, you will be of the most assistance to birthing a new world. Life feels real. It feels solid and it is, but it's also an illusion that you have the power to change waiting within you.

We have been fighting a war in our cosmic collective. This war was cyclical, as is all of creation, but we are now coming to a new cycle. It is an opportunity where the world will shift and each of us can choose what we do with this reintegration of our divinity here on earth. We have been fighting shadow forces who have tried to enslave and overtake this Matrix. This has all been apart of the game, but now the tides will begin to turn as the outdated Matrix built on oppression, suffering, and learning in density is disbanded, and the light takes power on this earth once again.

The shadow forces which inhabited our earth took power by circulating massive amounts of negativity through the matrix, cultivating false histories, religious dogma, media manipulations, and hiding the information humanity required to remember their spiritual roots. Without those roots they become stagnate. They used nefarious spiritual methods to monopolize the energies around our core resources, such as our food supplies, water sources, banking systems, entertainment industries and governmental infrastructures. To be clear, I am not saying that every person associated with those fields is possessed by some dark force, but rather that these are platforms the shadow forces used throughout this experiment to create negativity on earth.

A response to shadow forces is apart of our experiment, but now the karmic wheel of earth is being balanced and the powers that be will fall or transform anew. This doesn't mean it will happen overnight. We still have lessons in this chaos, but the more we cater to our spiritual growth on a personal level the more our collective journey will accelerate.

The cycle of shadow being in power on earth is coming to an end. That denser energy is being recycled and transmuted as we speak. We are being called to stand, to act and awaken. You were sent here because your essence is necessary and significant to the changes we are undergoing. You can choose how you use the gift of this life experience. The energy is being made available to us, but it is us who must choose to use it, or it will pass on by.

All is possible, this is a virtual reality. Anything can be created, and can come to pass, but that doesn't necessarily mean it's "easy" to create. In order to see true results, it is important you dedicate yourself to the relationship with your spirit and thus All That Is. Spend time mastering that relationship, cultivating awareness, nurturing your beliefs, choosing actions that are oriented in the light and this energy will yield many miraculous rewards for you.

Many energetic beings exist in dimensions that are unseen to us and assist in the manifestation of this Matrix. We are not alone here. We are being assisted in this shift by unseen armies summoned by our soul collective's call. Dream big. Go after what you want, and know you can have it. Know that this is a game and now you are learning the rules. Use them to your benefit and create all that your soul desires. It doesn't matter where you are or who you've been; you can do and be anything you wish; we just have to be willing and set the intention to move forward, take action with inspiration and follow our hearts.

YOUR ARMY OF LIGHT

We have all come to this earth with a team of "guides" or "unseen friends," who influence the path of our physical experience. These are close friends of your "Higher Self," your divine counterpart, who you really are. The earthly self, the human mind, is a fabricated identity for this grand experiment. Your Higher Self is the aspect of your soul that is ascended, that is still connected to the divine Source with no illusions of separation. You are their Avatar: a piece of themselves they sent in the form of your spirit to be apart of this shift.

You have an army of light at your side, and there is no separation between them and the Source of unconditional love. They do not suffer from smaller denser human emotions, judge you or seek to harm you. They wish only for you to be happy, connected and at peace. While that is their ultimate wish they cannot intervene if we do not ask, for as I said, free will is sacred. It is therefore important to call upon your armies, your highest most ascended self, and ask them to guide your experience toward your greatest good. To them, you are a bright spirit who is mature and responsible enough to create and seek for yourself. They are not forceful, but do wish to connect with us, so that we may evolve and ground more light into this earth.

I could hear her when I was younger trying to keep me out of trouble, the wise whisper in the back of my mind. This was my Higher Self. I often heard her, though I didn't always listen. In fact, I would usually go running in the opposite direction—but I could still hear her nonetheless. She was always whispering, waiting patiently for me to make the decisions to start my true path. I describe her in the feminine because that is how she has appeared to me, but your Higher Self has no gender. They are energy, but show themselves to us in ways we will accept or understand.

Though I first heard them through visions and words in my mind, our guides speak to us in many ways other than sight or sound. They speak to us through our art, they speak to us through our feelings, in our excitement, and our dreams of the future. They speak to us through Synchronicity, which Carl Jung defined as a meaningful coincidence. Signs, omens, intuitive hunches, chance encounters, numbers showing up repeatedly, perhaps you hear a certain song over and over again or look at the clock at an interesting time such as 11:11 or 12:34. These are all ways Spirit and your guides are letting you know "We are with you, and you are not alone."

Developing a conscious relationship with your Higher Self will be the foundation with which you build the rest of your spiritual path. Through meditation and various practices covered in the coming chapters you can work on strengthening your connection and accelerate the process of "blending," pulling your divine energy into your earth body so that, in this lifetime or those to follow, you may be fully integrated with your Higher Self in the physical. When you are able to ground and integrate that connection your life will steadily improve and become inherently magic because you will be emitting a higher vibration.

Everything is energy, therefore, everything is vibration. This idea is not new. Think of microwaves, radios, wi-fi, even television. You know these waves exist but you cannot see them in a physical sense. We are all connected vibrationally and moving to elevate our vibration as a collective. Every piece of this universe moves and vibrates at a different rate. Emotions that are closer to the energy of unconditional love are "high vibration," joy, love, bliss, compassion, gratitude. These are vibrations that are close to the divine, therefore they are powerful and bring both the person allowing them and the world around them profound healing and abundance. Negative emotions such as anger, fear or apathy are "low vibration" and can be stagnating if experienced too often. Accelerating the blending process means you are calling more of your light and yielding it so it can be grounded to manifest abundance in your life. You are taking the steps necessary to deepen your relationship with your Higher Self, to create an intimacy, and begin integrating and letting go of the various aspects of your ego and shadow-self, a process I will speak more of in the following chapter. With any spiritual aspiration, intention is the most important aspect of your process.

We are all figuring this out together, both in Spirit and on the physical plane of existence, all doing our best to support our soul mission and divine purpose in life. A large part of their spiritual purpose is to love and protect you. They want to establish an intimacy with all of us, and they love to communicate, whether it be through words, symbols, inspiration or experience.

During the beginning of my awakening, after nights of visceral meditation communicating with my guides, I would often be brought to tears at the immense love and understanding they provide for us. After feeling alone for so long, I realized how truly cared for and protected I was. How in my most shameful and downtrodden moments, they showed me love and unconditional grace. Like growing pains, allowing the love was a process, because when you have shut yourself down to love and you are still in the hardwired programs of the ego, it is difficult to allow yourself to be nurtured. Love feels foreign and it is also the ultimate healer, so the more love I allowed into my being, the more aspects of my ego were unearthed for me to process.

Your Higher Self holds all of your collective soul experiences, abilities, information and knowledge. As the blending process deepens you can have access to all of the different aspects of your divine inner self. We are beings made up of many dimensions, and have experienced many lifetimes—past life memories will often rise to the surface that are in need of healing, processing, or revealing. Ask your Higher Self to guide you through this process, and lead you to a healer or teacher that may assist you through anything in your personal multi-verse that is difficult to grasp or understand on your own. Affirm this healer or teacher's intentions to be for your highest good and the highest good of All That Is—though beware of putting people on pedestals. No one's teachings or belief system should ever supersede your own truth. Healers and teachers are just people and should not be held on a level above you.

Listen to your intuition. Your guides will make miracles happen in your life with dedication to this path. They will always come from a place of humility and love as Spirit does not see itself above or below us. They know that we are all one, and each one of us is sacred and cherished through the eyes of the divine.

Just because they are not in the physical does not make them any less real. What is tangible is their love and ability to assist, guide, orchestrate and create with us. Their perspective holds access to more than we in our physical existence can comprehend. They hold great wisdom for us to tap into and channel into our reality. It is they who have led you to the reading of these pages and whatever other spiritual explorations you are inspired to initiate. In the beginning, they would say "We are in the wind little one, feel us in the wind, feel us all around you." They have never stopped guiding us through this and every cycle of karmic density. They say it's time to let the pain go, and walk forward into a new beginning: connected, united, healed and free.

YOUR UNDERWORLD

We all have an underworld, parts of ourselves that we are not yet conscious of, that we have chosen to work with in this lifetime. The ego is your human programming and sense of self. It is the "rational mind" and allows you to do things like eat, drive, brush your teeth, not take candy from strangers and look both ways before you cross the street. Its origin and intention is survival. It's trying to keep you safe from any perceived threats of harm or pain and will use any means necessary to keep you in your illusion. Your shadow is where the ego hides all the parts of you that it has deemed undesirable and therefore, represses out of your conscious awareness. Memories, beliefs, behaviors, unattractive emotions, unresolved trauma or anything too emotionally daunting for the ego to comprehend, is waiting to be processed and released from the shadow self.

The problem with the modern ego is that it is overwhelmed and overworked. From early on we are fed fearful information from mass media and the rest of society. Combine that with the fact that many of us are carrying trauma from this life or others in our DNA, creating a sort of "soul-PTSD," which has inundated much of our global population with depression and/or anxiety. We live in an ego-centric society. People are addicted to being seen, validated, praised. We have forgotten our true divine nature and seek value in the external world.

The ego wishes you to stay small in its parameters of comfort and it can be dark, manipulative, crude or strange in the name of that mission. Whatever it can do to keep you stagnate—for it feels that it is protecting you from the unknown. The ego thinks that by distracting you, it won't have to deal with what is really fueling the flux of your emotions. Many walk around with guilt or confusion of all the strange thoughts rattling around in their minds, but when you have learned the nature of the ego, you can detach. Instead of being ashamed and accrediting your shadow to some false story trying to sell you on your own unworthiness, you can choose to let it go, to see it for what it really is, and allow it to pass through you, rather than rooting within you further. Negativity can be difficult to navigate but as you train yourself to the process of letting go, strengthening your vibration, accelerating the blending process with your Higher Self, you will climb to new energetic heights, and in doing so you will transform your reality.

When parts of the shadow are acknowledged they are then able to be released or processed. Clearing away various aspects of the shadow simply requires we look at ourselves honestly and give love to all of the parts inside of us the ego has deemed "unlovable." That we bear witness to all aspects both dark and light, not in judgment, but with compassion and an intention of awareness. What we resist will persist, meaning the more we try to fight the shadow the more power it has over you and your life. The harder we push to repress our shadow aspects, the harder they push back into our awareness. Create a safe space within yourself where you can look freely at your shadow. Ask yourself, "What am I afraid of? What am I ashamed of? What makes me insecure? What makes me angry, and why? What am I hiding from myself or the world?" Something magic happens when you can own all that you are. You can begin to forgive those aspects and eventually even rise above them. Boldly love your "Dark Side." Understand that when the shadow is integrated in your conscious reality, it becomes a source of great power, individuality and creativity.

People who are possessed by their ego are trapped in a state of perpetual discontent and desire. There is no peace, as the ego is always seeking. Whether it be for something it has attached desire to or validation from some external source. They are self absorbed and it can be draining to be in their presence. They can be consumed by material gain or superficial interests. To the ego, it is always someone else's fault. It wishes to absolve itself from personal responsibility, therefore it blames some external source for its various woes and negative situations.

People possessed by their ego are rarely able to accept responsibility or admit wrongdoing. They have beliefs of superiority or superciliousness. Simply put, they act as if they are better than other people. They want to be special and are often overbearing in proving it to you. For, in truth, they do not believe it themselves, and are stuck perpetually attempting to prove their value. The ego wants to keep you in judgment, so that you will stay on the surface of human experience. It wants you bored, vapid and complaining. It lacks self awareness and will be triggered by the shadow aspects in others that match its own. We are all reflecting each other. When you experience strong feelings of frustration, annoyance or judgment, ask yourself, why? What emotion is triggering you that you can find in yourself to call to awareness? When you can forgive and transmute your resentments, you are able to see those people and yourself for that matter, through the eyes of unconditional love. It takes a conscious person to turn the looking glass inward instead of projecting their shadow onto others and the world around them.

The core of the ego is selfishness. It is constantly aware of, worried about, and trying to elevate itself. It wonders what people are thinking about it, and creates false stories to perpetuate anxieties about things that don't really exist. The ego lives out its own soap opera and attaches itself to everything, spewing all of its negativity and hitching you along for the ride. It's the two year old in your brain trying to control everything and throwing tantrums when it doesn't get its way. The ego will do what it can to derail your process of spiritual growth, to protect you from what it has tried to avoid. This is why many who begin meditation and spiritual work will stop early on. Thoughts like, "I just can't meditate" or "It's not working anymore," will creep into your mind because the ego is trying to convince you to give up and stay in its parameters of comfort. It strives to keep you in martyrdom, blame, anger, pain, fear, victim-hood, for this is how it survives.

We all have our internal duality of the conscious and unconscious. This is a part of our journey here, dissolving and elevating passed these egoic aspects hidden in the shadow of our underworld. The shadow is a collective energy, as well as a personal one. The light workers who are here now have volunteered to work with the pieces which have drowned out the light in this world, so that they may alchemize (transmute) those aspects within themselves, and our collective may prosper. It is what we have been doing since the dawn of time—experiencing and collecting shadows during our various incarnations in this world, so that we may one day release, transmute and heal them.

Be aware of the "Spiritual Ego." Sometimes people who embark on the spiritual path fall into the trap of thinking that because they walk this path in a specific way, they are better than or more important than those who do not. It is often subtle (sometimes not), but it is just another level of the ego's ability to slither into our belief system. Everyone is on the spiritual path. We are just in different phases and expressions of it. Humility is the backbone of true power. When I accept that I will never know all things, I am free. The ego has enemies, Spirit does not. The ego is separation. Spirit is all things. The ego is illusion. Spirit is truth.

I repeat this mantra often "Spirit relieve me of my ego. Relieve me of my resistance." I'll say it many times throughout the day as a reminder to be conscious of where my thoughts and intentions are coming from. This is a world of illusions. When you are able to look at parts of yourself that are still unconscious, you are taking your power back from your ego mind and shadow self. The process of dissolving these parts can feel confusing and even uncomfortable at times, for the ego is attached to these negative aspects of your psyche and will fight to your dying breath to defend itself in its righteousness. When you stop fighting the ego and allow the pain of whatever is beneath it to be heard, the pain will eventually release. You will be wiser, stronger and grateful for the experience.

If you have experienced deep trauma this process may seem especially daunting. Try not to be afraid of your pain. It's hard to feel all of our emotions and let them go, rather than pushing them down, numbing them or locking them away. Don't be afraid to ask for help.

When you've been hurt, it can seem like it's going to last forever. Sometimes you want to throw everything away, and voices scream in your head to make it end. You wonder when you'll stop crying, when you'll stop being afraid, when it'll get better. You may then get angry and want revenge, to hurt others the way you've been hurt, or call yourself weak, and punish yourself further for the trauma you've experienced. That's okay.

It's perfectly fine to unravel, to be angry, to fall flat on your face. What matters is that you stand back up, that even in the hardest moments, the darkest nights of the soul, you fight, because you are a warrior. All of your battles have prepared you for the lessons and dreams you intended before embarking on this earthly journey, so use your shadow! Be an emotional alchemist and turn it into the fuel for your dreams.

When you are opening to Spirit and remembering all that you are, your ego will do whatever it can to impede the process, especially when you are on the brink of a spiritual breakthrough. Don't believe the voice in your head that speaks as a critic or fear monger. Take your power back from your underworld and shine your light like the beacon you've always intended to be.

Underworld Invocation:

I invoke my highest most ascended self to lead me through the various levels of my unconscious thoughts, emotions, beliefs, behaviors and memories which are no longer serving my highest good. Lead me through my underworld safely, and show me how to let go of aspects within me I no longer have use for. Teach me how to love all of me, and send love to all parts of my being which I have turned away from. I release all shame, fear, jealousy, envy, resentment, guilt, victimhood and martyrdom that keeps me in density, that I am ready to let go of at this time. In the event that I must travel deeper into the unseen worlds to find the answers I seek, may I be led to a shadow healer who can guide me through this experience. I forgive myself, my shadow, my ego, and align myself with the highest good of All That Is. By my own free will, in gratitude and so it is.

Reflection Questions:

Reflection questions will be scattered throughout the book.

Use them as you are inspired to do so.

They are not meant to be quiz like, but rather a resource for

questions you can ask yourself when venturing to the realms

within, whether integrating them in your meditations, using them

as journaling prompts or just for casual reflection.

Underworld reflection Questions:

What am I afraid of and why?
What makes me feel insecure and why?
What emotions within me do I most try
to hide from?
Where can I send myself more love?
What qualities in other people make me angry?
Where can I find those qualities in myself?
What am I ashamed of and why?
What are my darkest desires?
Am I being my authentic self or
creating an identity to please the world?
What triggers me?
Is there any pain from my past which
I have not been able to face?
Am I loving ALL of me?

YOUR POWER

You are a thread of the divine tapestry led by our Creators on a perpetual journey of discovery, growth and magic. You have tremendous power inside of you. This power stems from your light, and your light comes from the stars. You are never alone. You are sacred, and your presence in this time is vital for all that is to come. Armed with this knowledge, you are standing in the power of your spirit, and therefore, feeling worthy of all that life has to offer you. Emotions are power. It is energy directed and constantly in motion. Unconditional love is the most powerful emotion that exists. When you stand in that power and let it emanate from the core of your being, life will open and transform before your very eyes.

We give our power away by attaching to other people or situations with energetic cords of fear, frustration, anger, blame and so on. These emotions interrupt your flow of unconditional love from our creators, giving your life force away to whatever has catalyzed your negative emotion. This is nothing to feel ashamed of because we have come for an emotionally varied experience, and the process of learning to let go of these emotions isn't always easy. It is time for us take back the knowledge of who we really are and what we are worthy of, so that we may transform this world collectively.

People standing fully in their power live in stark contrast to those still very much possessed by the ego. They need no external validation, thus they don't need anything from you. When you are communicating with someone in their power, it feels warm, relaxed and genuine. They aren't trying to emotionally manipulate you into some sort of endgame because they are complete, and in joy unto themselves. They aren't afraid of who they are and don't need to control the world to feel at peace. This is the essence of true freedom, unconditional joy, happiness in each and every moment. They are kind, inclusive, and they listen to you because they aren't lost obsessing over what they are going to say next or how you are perceiving them. They are interested in you rather than trying to be interesting TO you. They allow the world and themselves to be free and unconstrained, which is why they are so pleasant to be around.

When you believe in yourself, in what you're doing and what you're saying, others will stop and listen. It is receivable. It is grounded. People can feel the power that is emanating from your confidence. You feel at peace, because you are not giving your joy away to fear or any other negativity. You feel safe because you are allowing the love in that says "You are good, you are worthy, and you are unconditionally loved." It is a process learning to let that voice in, especially because many of us have accumulated a great deal of negative emotional programs. Just keep pointing in a gentler direction and soon the current of your thoughts will transform and you will stand further in your divine light.

When you are in your power, your dreams feel that much more attainable, because you are not giving any heed to the anxiety trying to convince you otherwise. This doesn't mean that you have no fear or ego buried in the recesses of your mind—it means you don't let them attach to your perspective. You don't identify with and own these insecurities, allowing them to dictate your experience. Instead of allowing it to root or siphon away your power, you simply let it wash through you. Anyone you admire, anyone who has achieved greatness, has met with resistance on their path. They have wrestled with the fear and insecurities that plague our inner most desires, but they never gave it enough power to keep them from success.

One of the first steps in taking your power back is convincing yourself that you are worthy of it. You are worthy of joy, of safety, love, abundance and fulfilment.

We live in a society that likes to glorify suffering, that pushes ideals of sanctity in self sacrifice. In reality this is just martyrdom, another facet of the ego. Martyrdom is tricky because some of us have been taught that we should serve others above ourselves, that true selflessness brings salvation. Some have painted our creators into vengeful creatures who wish for us to suffer and seek our oppression. I respectfully disagree. The divine loves us and wishes us all to live in peace, joy and salvation. That being said, it is our responsibility to step into our power and affirm that we are worth the infinite nature and abundance of divine love, and therefore choose it, for they cannot do this for us.

Here is an affirmation to begin the journey of taking back your spiritual power. Saying it out loud makes it that much more powerful. The stronger the emotions behind it, the more energetic weight it carries:

Power Affirmation:

I am One with God, Goddess, All That is. I stand fully in the power of my most ascended self. I call my power back from wherever I have given it away, to any person, place or situation in this timeline and dimension and all others which my energetic expression has been manifest past, present or future. I ground my power into the womb of Mother Earth so she may grow and nurture my light. I am grounded and in tune fully with my absolute spiritual power, presence and divine identity. I Am.

By my own free will, in gratitude, and so it is.

POWER REFLECTION QUESTIONS:

Do I stand often in
my spiritual power?
Do I give my power away
to the negativity in my life?
Am I dominated
or dominating
in my relationships?
Do I try to make
myself small
or unthreatening to
please people?
Do I stand my
ground and
do what is
best for me?
What brings me
the most joy?
Do I feel whole
within myself?

Do I overcompensate
for my insecurities by
attempting to seem
larger than life or better than
others?
Does it feel okay to be alone?
Am I satisfied with my own
presence?
Do I believe my needs are
less important than
others?
Am I self sacrificing
my joy for vampiric
entities in my life?
Am I caring for
my self enough?
Can I say no to other
people's demands on my
time and energy?

MEDITATION

Meditation is the doorway to your internal universe. It is the key and the opening for you to connect, contact and blend with the realms of Spirit. When I first began meditating my mind was not a pleasant place to be, and it wasn't looking to be slowed down, which meant looking at all the density I had accumulated—it meant being alone with myself instead of hiding in my static. I found tools that assisted in my process like "binaural beats," which assist the brain in entering a meditative state, or various types of guided journeys, but most importantly, I just kept doing it. Every day, as often as I could bare. Slowly, it got better, easier. Then the changes started manifesting in my life and I came to realize how powerful the process of training the mind and nurturing the spirit could be.

If you go online you will find countless sources and studies on why meditation is not only useful on the spiritual plane but also in the physical realm. When you meditate you are doing a multitude of positive things. First, you are learning to control your mind. When you gain control over your mind, rather than your mind controlling you, your path will change and bloom. You will have taken your power back from your thoughts, and you will be able to decide what channel they are on and therefore what will eventually manifest. In meditation, you are pulling your mind away from the static and back to the present, to the breath or whatever you choose to be your focus.

Second, you are going inward and beginning the communication with your inner void and self. You are clearing a way through the static of your mind for the divine energy to be siphoned, received and grounded. Your spirit cannot get through the static of your mind if it is never in stasis. Spirit needs stillness to become comfortable and heard. When you are in meditation, you are allowing the divine energy to flow through you, releasing resistance and pent up emotion and therefore raising your vibration.

When you are always in motion, and you don't have a practice that encourages discipline, your energy will be all over the place. You are probably not grounded, so your life will lack balance. Meditation gave me what I was always looking for, a connection—more meditation, more release, more power. I was calling my light forward and it was fueling and altering my experience. For the first time, I was feeling peace and gratitude on a daily basis. The world became crisper, alive. It was as if all that static was a filter and when I wiped it away, I could appreciate all that was around me, thus attracting more things of that nature into my experience. Synchronicities were abundant. It was if the world was singing to me in a way I had never experienced before, save perhaps for some stolen glimpses into these higher dimensions via intoxication, but this was entirely different. This was pure. I inundated myself with information on meditation and the law of attraction. The more I practiced what I was learning, the more miraculous the results became.

All this being said, there are many ways and types of meditation. A lot of us have trouble jumping into closed eyed stationary meditations immediately. Coloring, drawing, reading, walking, dancing, all of these can be a meditation. In each moment you can be pointing your mind to the direction you wish it to function. In the end, you don't need anything fancy, even if it's just taking a couple of moments to yourself, a few deep breaths in the morning, and in times it starts to wander bringing your mind back to your breath. What you put into building the foundation of your spirituality is what you will yield from it. The more consistent you are on a daily basis with your meditation practice, the more expediently your progress will occur.

That being said it's also possible to meditate too much. It's not to be overdone as you can get lost in those worlds and begin neglecting or avoiding your physical experience. I like to do at least a solid hour a day, even if that is separated in thirty minute increments, one when I wake and one before I drift back into the world of dreams.

MUDRAS IN YOUR MEDITATIONS:

Mudras are posed hand gestures with ancient eastern roots. You can use mudras in your meditations to focus and attune your life force with a particular intention. In Sanskrit "mudra" translates to "gesture" "seal" or "mark." I like to use mudras in my meditations because I can feel the differences while performing the various gestures and have noticed a profound effect in my ability to deepen my meditative state since adopting the practice. Your hands are very connected to your "chi" or life force energy and directing them in certain mudras helps that energy to assimilate and flow within the body while "sealing" an intention. While there are mudras which make use of entire body movements, I have included only a few examples performed by the fingers and hands. However, if the tradition calls to you it is a topic that is certainly worth more in depth exploration. Here are a few of my favorite mudras to get you started:

Kubera Mudra:

Use this Mudra to focus your energy and bring your dreams into manifestation. Incorporate it into meditations where you are trying to set clear and strong intentions. Perfect for planting energetic seeds.

Ksepana Mudra:

This Mudra is for clearing yourself of any forms of negative energy. Feel all the energy you wish to release pouring out of your fingertips as you practice it. Great to use after going through a crowd, or interacting with energy you did not resonate with.

Lotus Mudra:

The Lotus Mudra will assist in opening your heart in all of its forms. It promotes compassion, forgiveness, and unconditional love. It also represents purity and transformation, like the lotus who is born from seed and darkness, and then grows into a majestic creation in contrast to all from which she came.

YOUR LITTLE ONE

Your heart is a world of its own and in the center of that world lives your little one, that curious, innocent, unconditionally loving part we all share in our earliest youth. Now is the time to seek them out. They may still be carrying wounds from long forgotten memories, even hidden away from you as a result. You may wonder where that part of you went and when exactly it went away. It's not gone, just hidden underneath the pain you haven't released, waiting patiently to be rediscovered. This isn't just for those with excessively traumatic childhoods, for many souls living on earth can be a traumatic affair, especially if their spirit is not accustomed to the dense energy here. I've never met a person that I think wouldn't benefit from some soothing of their inner little one.

As your mind develops, it rationalizes or represses the pain of youth, but your inner child is still carrying the trauma to this day, flooding you with fear and anxiety. Your Higher Self knows that these buried emotions will keep you tethered to the density in this world, so it attempts to create situations that catalyze the very pain you run away from, hoping you'll eventually just give in and cry it out.

Most of us have experienced some degree of trauma by an early age. This trauma opens a pathway for shadow to be sustained and developed. The pain breaks off a piece of that child's soul, temporarily suspending it in that darker dimension, which translates to your current reality as some kind of emotional unrest. There are lessons in even the darkest of tragedies. You chose the shadow, just as you chose the light, but now it's time to let go of any weight that inner little one may still be harboring.

Visit with your inner child in meditation. Call them forward and allow them to be heard. Hold them. Allow them to release harbored emotions that depend on you for sustenance. Be the protector you didn't have. Create a world where they feel nurtured and safe. If you are someone with anxiety, this could be a great assistance for you, as it was for me. It's the scared child that grew up too fast, that's still trying to find the love it wasn't provided. My inner child gets exhausted with this world. She has no patience for this darkness and, frankly, would rather sleep. However, I have worked on creating a sacred space for her in the multidimensional world of my soul and since then my anxiety has decreased dramatically. Ask them what they need and listen. You might not have been heard as a child and it's important to give yourself that gift. If you allow them to express their pain, to release pent up emotions that they couldn't make sense of at the time, you can then create a new world and realize their consolation as your own. The relationship with your inner child never ends, they will always be a part of you. If you create an intimacy and a solid foundation for that child now, it will carry lasting effects on your life.

Your opinion of your mother and father will be reflected in your relationship with the divine parental archetypes of our creators. If you had abusive parents, then healing and energetic separation should occur. Create new parents in this world you are visualizing. Create your ideal foundation and give that little one what they need. They deserve that; you deserve that. Spend time getting to know who that little spark is. Let their light shine and invigorate this world again.

Your inner child craves fun, adventure, silliness and joy, so after you get all that emotional sludge off, allow yourself these things because the fulfillment that comes from soothing the spirit will radiate from your experience and into All That Is. It's important to forget the world every once in a while and allow that inner little one to feel free.

Once your inner child feels safe, you will experience an elevated sense of peace. This is because you are no longer run by the wounds of childhood. When you were young you didn't have the capability to comprehend situations that make perfect sense to you now. You aren't weak for being affected, even if you feel like others have had it worse. Better or worse can't be applied to pain. Give the gift of attentive care that perhaps you weren't given in the beginning of your journey. Do this, and watch your relationship with the world blossom. Fight for your innocence, fight for that magic and creativity. Don't let the world dim your flame, or keep you in dark-

ness. You are magic. You are worthy, and you can change the world.

Inner Child Invocation:

I invite my little spark out to play.

I welcome your innocence, purity and creativity. I acknowledge your power, wisdom and light. I invite you to share any of your burdens and release all of your pain onto me. I will be strong for you, and allow you the space to breathe and feel heard. You are safe and protected. You are loved, and you are never alone. Show me how to live freely once again, to live purely for the joy of my experience. I ask my highest most ascended self to cleanse and bless my inner child, guiding me in nursing all wounds which need attention and creating a safe space for them within my soul.

By my own free will, in gratitude, and so it is.

INNER LITTLE ONE RELFECTION QUESTIONS:

How does my inner little
one feel right now?
What can I do to soothe
and relieve them?
How can I better hold space
for their experience?
Do I need to cry or let them
release through me?
Are there events and memories
from my childhood
which they could be
bearing the burden of?
What is a fun thing I can
add to my daily or weekly
routine which would make
my inner child happy?
Am I appreciating
and nurturing my
little spark?

CHAKRAS

Your chakras make up the basis of your energy body like the organs of your physical body. They work together and if one is not balanced then the whole system will be affected. Ask your Higher Self to begin the process of balancing your chakras, aligning them with their highest light and releasing all density that is keeping them out of balance. The first step is always asking; intention is key. Ask for what you want, in faithful trust, and gradually, as you allow it, it will be done.

You are a universe. Your chakras are the planets of your "Soul System," realms of energetic coding which work together to manifest the totality of you and your reality. Each chakra is a world unto itself, each containing multitudes of information, dimensions, and various forms of energetic expression. Beliefs, memories, contracts, traumas, identity perspectives are all held in the chakra system and this dictates how you and your life manifest in the physical world. Whatever woes you may be experiencing have a root somewhere in your chakra system. Heal the energy and you will release the dis-ease. All that is manifest in the physical world is first birthed in the nonphysical. Explore your inner worlds and focus on bringing balance to your energetic anatomy for this will manifest profound healing for your self and the world.

As you heal blockages or imbalances in the chakras it will reflect in your reality. Feed them with affirmations, visualizations and attention. Fill them with positive energy and ask your Higher Self to help you unearth any blockages you may want to release and heal, so that you can use that energy once again for your highest good.

The following pages will summarize the seven most notable chakras (though we have many more) that can act as a foundation to understanding and healing your chakra system.

Root Chakra

Your root chakra is your connection to Mother Earth and the foundation upon which you build the rest of your chakra system.

Balanced:
When your root chakra is in balance you will have no problems manifesting all of your survival needs. You will feel connected to the earth, to your body, and this experience will feel safe, fluid and provided for.

Overactive:
If your root chakra is creating excess energy you may be overly attached to the material world and believe that your worth stems from material gain. It can cause people to be controlling, rigid, irritable, angry, greedy and dependent on sources of safety and security.

Underactive:
In the event of an underactive root chakra you may have difficulties staying focused throughout your daily life, creating boundaries in relationships, manifesting basic survival needs, and feeling safe in your body. It can cause feelings of anxiety, loneliness, despair, depression or apathy.

Possible Blockages:
Fear, molestation or sexual abuse, being abandoned by mother or father, growing up in poverty, extreme bodily harm or illness, birth trauma, abusive parents, ancestral wounding

Healing Affirmation:
"I am safe. I am grounded. I am worthy. I am provided for. My foundation is strong and stable. I trust Mother Earth and embrace my experience with love and appreciation."

SACRAL CHAKRA

Your sacral chakra houses all of your creative energies, your beliefs about pleasure and sexuality and your emotional cords to other people.

Balanced:
When the sacral chakra is balanced, it will be easy for you to express your emotions, creations and sexuality. You will have a deep gratitude for your earthly experience and seek to embrace it wholeheartedly.

Overactive:
Excess energy in the sacral chakra can result in addictions to drama, substances, sex, attention or adrenaline. You will have difficulty setting boundaries and therefore may be carrying various people's toxic energy. It can also cause extreme mood swings, jealousy or manipulative thoughts and tendencies.

Underactive:
An underactive sacral chakra will make it difficult for you to receive pleasure, create the life and career you desire, and take care of the self. You may have fears or guilt surrounding sexuality, or feel like you are disconnected from your emotions and the world.

Possible Blockages:
Guilt, sexual or emotional abuse, unresolved feelings of rejection, ostracization from your peers, any unresolved trauma from your parents, drug or alcohol abuse (personal or familial), any trauma which caused you to attempt to disconnect or numb your emotions

Healing Affirmation:
"I am worthy of receiving pleasure, love and joy. I love to feel, and I embrace my emotions. I love my body, sexuality and the power of creation. I create fluidly with All That Is."

SOLAR PLEXUS CHAKRA

Your solar plexus chakra is the Sun of your "Soul System." It is the center of your sense of self, willpower and discipline.

Balanced:
A person with a balanced solar plexus chakra will have a strong sense of self and will not be easily swayed by the world around them. They will be respectful towards themselves and others and have little issue taking responsibility for their experience. They will be confident, self disciplined, passionate in their lives and usually have a clear life purpose.

Overactive:
When the solar plexus is working overtime you likely have an addiction to power and may feel superior to others. Explosive and controlling behaviors can manifest, and you will find it difficult to let loose or relax. You may see the world as a competitive game and will perpetually be trying to win against or upstage others. You may have an excessively rebellious side and enjoy the feeling of going against the grain.

Underactive:
An underactive solar plexus chakra will manifest in a person as a lack of willpower and self esteem. You will probably be someone who is overly focused on pleasing other people and will try to change in order to fit what you believe they desire from you. Not being connected to your power center can make one feel insecure, apathetic, depressed, indecisive or lonely.

Possible Blockages:
Shame, sexual abuse, repressive or abusive childhood, negative sense of self, abusive relationships, staying in situations we knew were not benefiting us

Healing Affirmation:
"I honor all that I am. I am strong, confident and full of grace. My power is infinite, and I feel it radiating inside me. I stand in the power of my Highest Self."

HEART CHAKRA

The heart chakra holds all of our attitudes, projections and beliefs about giving and receiving love, and it is where we integrate the understanding of our emotional connection to all things.

Balanced:
If your heart chakra is healthy and balanced, it will be easy for you to connect with the world and those close to you. You will radiate a light and compassionate energy, which people will flock to. You will feel harmonious connections in your relationships and find it effortless to give and receive love.

Overactive:
An overactive heart chakra can result in a person who uses love as a technique for manipulation rather than an unconditional gift. They will be possessive in relationships and may be considered overly sensitive or find it difficult to be emotionally honest with themselves and others.

Underactive:
A person with an underactive heart chakra may feel like a victim to their life and circumstances. They will find it incredibly difficult to express or receive love, compassion and care and can be cold or paranoid in relationships. They may suffer from depression and have a hard time allowing people to get close to them.

Possible Blockages:
Grief, being manipulated by parents or authority figures, loss, not receiving adequate care and love as a child, abusive relationships

Healing Affirmation:
"I am loved. I am wanted. I forgive myself and others for our shortcomings. I open myself to receive the love of All That is. I am compassionate, joyful and connected."

THROAT CHAKRA

Your throat chakra governs all forms of your expression
and communication.

Balanced:
A balanced throat chakra will make it easy for someone to express
their truth, beliefs, creations and ideas uninhibited by self doubt. It
will also make it possible for them to listen and hear people when
they are communicating. It results in honest and authentic people
who honor themselves and communicate what they desire with ease.

Overactive:
Excess energy in the throat chakra can result in people who don't
have the ability to listen and are biding time in conversations until it
is their turn to talk. They may be prone to gossipy or deceitful behaviors and find it difficult to be honest in expressing their truth. They
project a self righteous attitude onto the world and attempt to domi-
nate or overpower others.

Underactive:
Someone who has an underactive or shut down throat chakra will
hardly ever be heard speaking. They can be shy, introverted and
dishonest. They may feel anxious if expected to perform publicly and
can form drug or alcohol addictions that make them feel like they can
express themselves uninhibited by fear.

Possible Blockages:
Shame, deceit, growing up in a household where your truth or
creations were not valued or were shut down, excessively critical or
abusive childhood or relationship

Healing Affirmation:
*"My expressions are valuable. What I say and feel is sacred. I am
authentic and honest in my communications. I love to listen to others
and share my own expressions in return. I honor my truth."*

THIRD EYE CHAKRA

The third eye chakra is where you are able to see and perceive both the inner and outer worlds. Intuition and the ability to see your guides and Higher Self are governed here.

Balanced:
When a third eye chakra is active and balanced you flow with the cosmic waves of life, tapping into the universal guidance that surrounds us always. Synchronicity will be obvious in your experience and you will be able to access your psychic intuitive gifts easily. You will see the world for the whole picture rather than just through the intellect or rational mind.

Overactive:
If your third eye chakra is too open you can be prone to egomaniacal beliefs and behaviors and will be at risk of being overwhelmed by intuitive or psychic information that is not able to be understood or translated. They may be fanatical about religious beliefs and can be dominating towards people in their lives.

Underactive:
When the third eye is underactive you may be overrun by the intellect and not able to connect to the psychic or spiritual realms. You may be prone to feelings of paranoia and be easily confused or find it difficult to focus and see truth in your daily life.

Possible Blockages:
Fear of the unknown or your spiritual gifts, being raised in a particularly religious, dogmatic household, an unwillingness to look beyond the third dimensional experience

Healing Affirmation:
"I see clearly. My intuitive and psychic sight is open and balanced. I trust my divine intuition. I listen to the wisdom of my spirit. I am fully connected to my higher awareness and self."

CROWN CHAKRA

The crown chakra is your direct line to Source energy.
It is your center of divine knowing, reaching passed the intuitive
realms into direct connection and understanding of your oneness
with All That Is.

Balanced:
A balanced crown chakra results in a person who is fully connected and knowing of their connection to All That Is. They are a conduit for spiritual light and information and have a perpetual optimism, knowing that they are guided and protected in everything they do. If the lower chakra system is balanced the crown is able to activate and become privy to all universal knowledge.

Overactive:
An overactive crown chakra may result in psychotic behavior or episodes as well as bipolar mood swings. This person will often feel like they are floating away or feel disassociated from the world or their experience. They can have a hard time making decisions and overcompensate in the lower chakras resulting in overly materialistic or earthly based dependencies.

Underactive:
When the crown chakra is underactive it can result in people with addictions to spirituality and extremely depressive states. They will feel empty and may not have very much motivation to continue living. They will be run primarily by the intellect and find it difficult to think "out of the box."

Possible Blockages:
Addictions or attachments to the third dimensional world, an unbalanced lower chakra system, repressive childhood environment, fanatical or religious upbringing

Healing Affirmation: *"I am one with All That Is. I am divinity incarnate. I listen to the knowing of my Spirit. I am open to the wisdom of Source energy. I am."*

CHAKRA REFLECTION QUESTIONS:

 Am I trusting? Am I allowing my divine knowing to flow through me? Do I feel connected to the higher planes of this Universe?

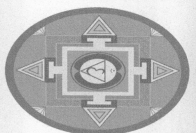 Do I listen to my intuition? Am I conscious of all the messages Spirit is trying to send me? Am I holding rigid beliefs that are blocking my spiritual gifts?

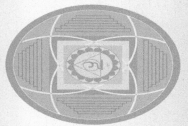 Do I express myself with honesty and authenticity? Am I allowing myself to be heard? Do I allow my creative energy to express?

 Am I able to give and receive love with ease? Have I let my heart close up in response to past heart break? Do I feel connected to the world around me?

 Do I stand in my power? If not, where am I giving it away? Do I feel worthy of success? Am I joyful?

 Do I embrace my creative inspiration? Am I allowing myself to receive pleasure? How do I feel about my sexuality?

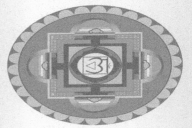 Am I connected to Mother Earth? Do I feel safe? What is my foundation built upon?

CRYSTALS & CHAKRAS

You can use crystals to assist with your chakra healing. Carry them around with you, or incorporate them into your meditative practice. Ask your Higher Self to guide you to the stones that would benefit you most. Here are a few options according to which chakra you're trying to work with:

Crown Chakra: Ajoite, Amethyst, Angel Aura Quartz, Black Merlinite, Celestite, Cryolite, Herkimer Diamonds, Lemurian Seeds, Sugilite, White Aventurine.

Third Eye Chakra: Amethyst, Apophyllite, Azurite, Blue Tourmaline, Indigo Kyanite, Lapis Lazuli, Labradorite, Moladvite, Rainbow Moonstone, Sodalite, Sugilite.

Throat Chakra: Aquamarine, Lapis Lazuli, Sodalite, Apatite, Kyanite, Azurite, Angelite, Labradorite, Blue Howlite, Blue Quartz, Blue Tiger's Eye.

Heart Chakra: Jade, Green Tourmaline, Rose Quartz, Emerald, Peridot, Garnite, Malachite, Green Calcite, Chrysocolla, Rhodochrosite, Amazonite, Turquoise.

Solar Plexus: Citrine, Yellow Quartz, Tigers Eye, Yellow Tourmaline, Yellow Jade, Rutilated Quartz, Honey Quartz, Septarian, Amber.

Sacral Chakra: Citrine, Moonstone, Amber, Honey Calcite, Rhyolite, Coral, Orange Calcite, Orange Adventurine.

Root Chakra: Red Carnelian, Black Tourmaline, Aragonite, Bloodstone, Red Jasper, Obsidian, Garnite, Red Calcite, Agite, Hematite, Smokey Quartz, Pyrite, Mookaite

Make sure to research the kind of care and cleansing that is required for the crystals you're drawn to, so you can keep them at optimum health and performance.

KARMA

Karma

Karma is cosmic law. Its mechanism leads our universal education and is built into the fabric of our reality. As the soul travels, choices are made. With every choice, there is a direction born. For every action there is a reaction. For every cause, there is an effect. The place you are in now is a culmination of every choice, action and intention you have made since the dawn of your soul's exploration. These factors combined form your karmic path, which is all you will learn and all you will do as you walk back discovering who you truly are. Karma is not a punishment. It is precise, and it is fair. Though that is sometimes hard to grasp immersed in this three dimensional experience, especially in a world with such widespread suffering and corruption, we have chosen our path, and we have done so for a reason.

Though the human mind may reject this experience as something you would not wish for yourself, your Higher Self has chosen every lesson with care, and it hasn't chosen anything you can't handle. As you develop, your karma (all you have to learn here) releases and you grow closer to the Source of All That Is. Karma is malleable and moves with the consciousness of the now, meaning it is dictated not just by the past but in each present moment by your place of understanding and intention. What is karma trying to teach us? Love. At the core of this mechanism is a guiding subtle force attempting to teach us all to be more compassionate and connected.

I am a survivor of sexual assault. Coming to terms with the fact that I chose those experiences was, in particular, not easy for me. Learning that some higher part of me made that decision—that I could have been on the other side of anything like what I experienced was almost impossible to comprehend. However, as I came to discover that we have all lived hundreds of thousands of lives, each through a different lens, it became the understanding that aided me in forgiving those I felt had tarnished me. We have all been on the other side of our tragedies. As difficult as that may be to hear, we have sought to experience all perspectives. I saw that the beings who abused me were just Angels covered in shadows. They were playing a part in my story. Our world is a simulation, a play we have all volunteered for and all parts are necessary to the whole. I'm not going to invite them over for dinner or anything, and it doesn't excuse their behavior, but I have forgiven them and therefore freed myself from the shackles of that experience.

This planet has been cyclically purging out layers of karmic density for centuries. We have been working out the lessons of the collective shadow created by the legacy of our choices, and we now walk with open eyes into a time of light. Chaos surrounds and systems will fall, but we are being led to a new world. The karma of this planet is being purged expediently, and the evolution to spiritual grace is steadfast in its birth. We have learned enough in suffering and we are finally being allowed to let go of the old dense mediums of karmic education and graduate further into our ascension. All that is required to speed the release of your karmic density is to let go and learn to love. We are going through a cosmic reset, and it will be easier than ever to release the shadows and return completely to the light.

This world is a dream, albeit a convincing one, and it is constantly showing you signs even when you aren't aware of them. You are a detective. Immerse yourself in the mystery that Spirit is weaving for you, the clues your Higher Self leaves to guide where you are meant to go and what you are meant to learn. Life is a gift even when it seems like a curse because you are being guided to your ultimate purpose. Nothing happens by accident. The more you dedicate yourself to the path of self-remembrance and clearing away those karmic densities, the more clarity, synchronicity and magic will flood your experience.

If you are out there and experiencing a difficult situation, know that you are a powerful creator and you chose a lifetime with many lessons because you wanted to grow into something magnificent. You knew you could handle it. So much of my adolescence was spent in anger toward "God," or whatever power had thrust my trauma upon me. Now I know I was never forced to go through this life, or any life for that matter. I chose my experiences because I wanted to grow, and I wanted to do it fast. If you are here, you have answered the call to be here and usher in this ascension. You had big plans, and it's time to get started!

Karma Cleanse Affirmation:

I begin the process of cleansing and purging my karmic slate now. I release any cords of karmic density that have kept me tethered to this earth's karmic wheel back into Mother Earth for transmutation in any and all dimensions and time lines where my expression has been manifest, past, present or future. I walk fully and completely into my divine power, light and ultimate destiny.

By my own free will, in gratitude, and so it is.

Karma Reflection Questions:

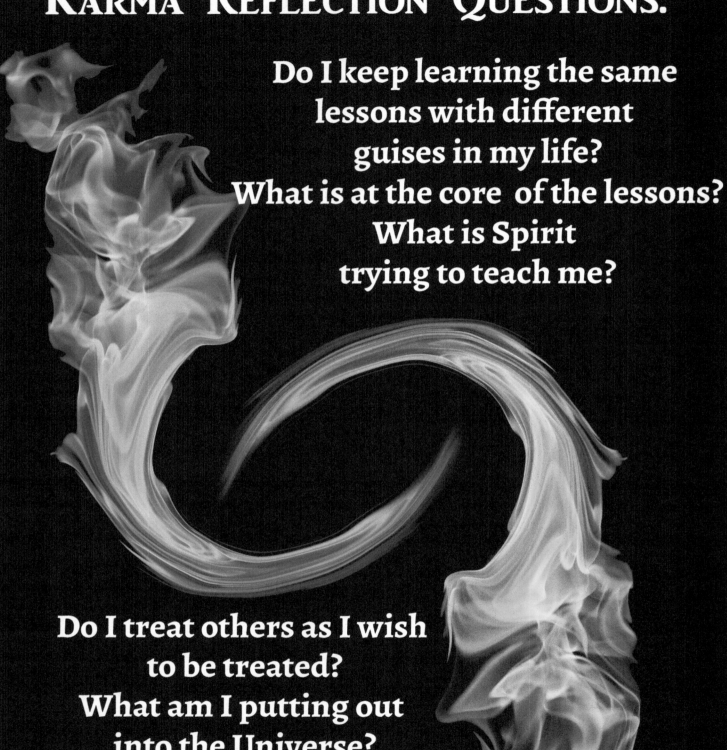

Do I keep learning the same
lessons with different
guises in my life?
What is at the core of the lessons?
What is Spirit
trying to teach me?

Do I treat others as I wish
to be treated?
What am I putting out
into the Universe?
How am I serving this
world with love?
And how may I do so more often?

Karmic Goodies:

The trick to good deeds is to do them for the sake of doing them, rather than a belief that you will get something in return. The fact that you can give at all is the gift. Giving feels good, and it always circles back eventually just like all the energy you send out. That being said, here are a few simple ways you can give in your daily life, opportunities for you to spread good karmic energy into the Universe.

1. Smile.
2. Listen intently when someone is opening up to you.
3. Go that extra mile for someone if they ask for your help.
4. Pay for the person's coffee in line behind you.
5. Call your parents, and ask about their day.
6. Hold the door open for the person behind you.
7. Pay for someone's expired parking meter.
8. Do the right thing, even if no one is watching.
9. Compliment a stranger.
10. Recycle!
11. Leave a sweet note in a public place for someone to find.
12. Volunteer for a cause.
13. Donate old clothes to a charity for those in need.
14. Buy a meal for a homeless person.
15. Make a special breakfast or dinner for your partner.
16. Return something you found that someone lost.

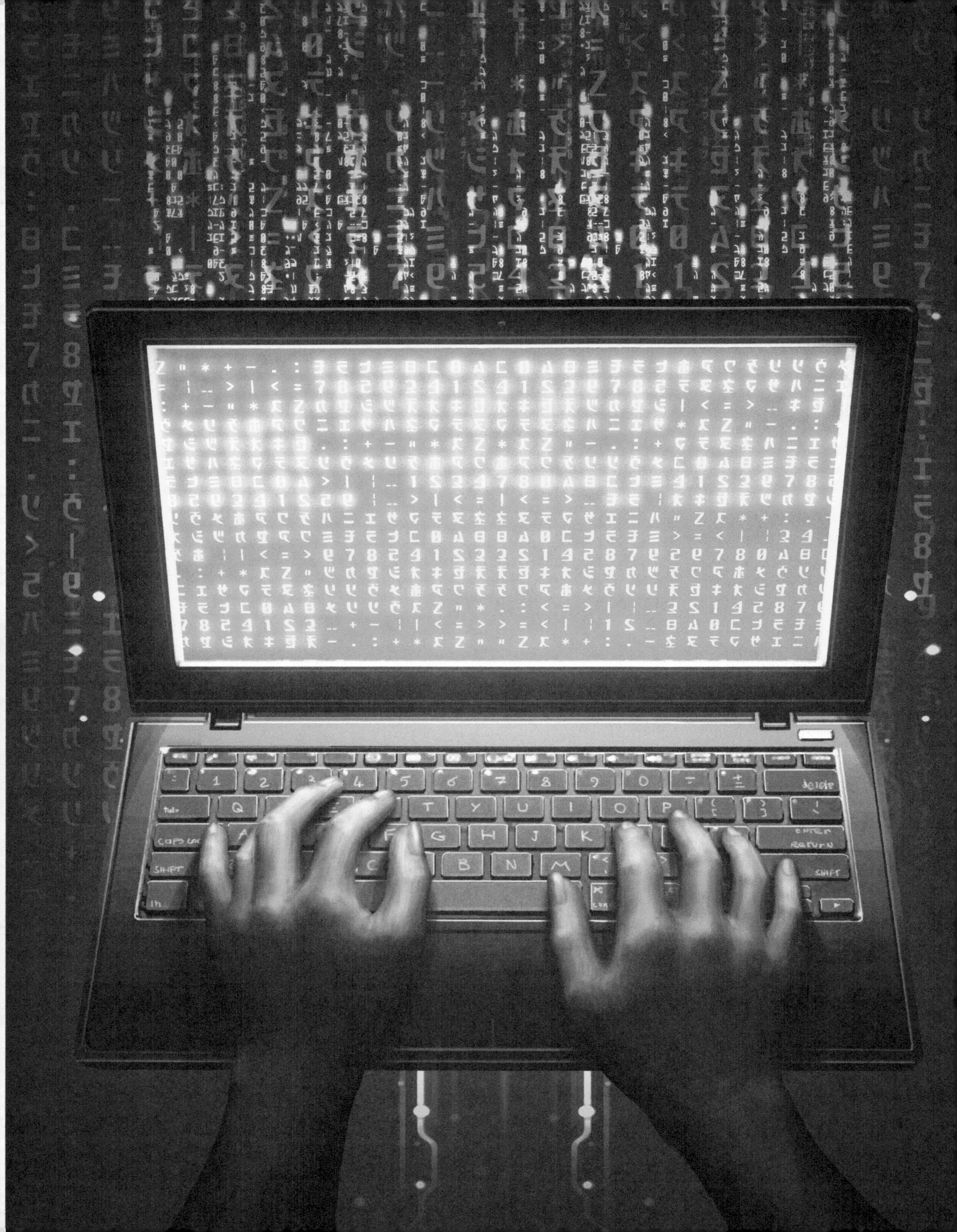

Programming your Matrix

As I said before, you create your reality with thoughts, beliefs, choices and actions. I have covered The laws of karma and free will bringing us now to the law of attraction. "That which is likened to itself will be drawn," meaning what you are, you will attract. You don't "use" or "harness" the law of attraction. It is a mechanism of this universe and is evident in all of creation.

In any given moment you are creating the reality around you. Some may say, "but I do not want this reality. I didn't choose this family, these hardships, this time, or this place." But you did. Throughout your soul's legacy, karmic choices and paths were embarked upon, avatars made manifest, and here you are. They wanted to learn something, and you are the vessel for that education. Now that you know that you are creating your reality, you have the power to change it and that is a blessed thing. So enjoy where you are, wherever that is, but know that it is just a moment in time, and you have the power to shape and sustain any future you desire. Everything is temporary. Change is the only constant.

When you begin to sustain a regular meditation practice, your repressed dense energy, which is in the way of your progression, will reveal itself for processing. It is showing itself to you to create and allow the release for your own benefit. This resistance may manifest in your emotions or may even catalyze situations in your life that will lead to a confrontation with your trauma. You are opening further spiritually, and your karmic lessons will accelerate, which means life may get chaotic before that which you are seeking can manifest. Don't get discouraged, look at each situation or emotion that arises as an opportunity to learn and move on to higher levels of consciousness. The more you are able to release, the more positive and effortless your life will become.

If you can match the emotion of the reality that you desire and fan the flames of that emotion, it has no choice but to eventually manifest. There are many ways to work with your emotional vibration and the law of attraction. From my experience, writing is a potent method and one I use on a daily basis. It may sound simple, but writing down what you want yields incredible power, and it is an important tool on the path to alchemizing your experience.

Writing a manifestation journal isn't much different than a regular journal entry. The only difference being the events that you are writing have not yet manifested in the physical. Your subconscious mind cannot tell the difference between that which you are experiencing, and that which you are "imagining" you are experiencing. Meaning it will create from what you feel within, not what is already physically manifested in your reality. Thus, writing it as if it has already happened will begin to sustain the emotion inside you. This will magnetize you and bring you closer to the reality that you ultimately seek. Understand, the words themselves don't really matter. It's the emotional response that the words illicit, the feeling that is emoted is what is pulling that desire closer. Have you ever lost yourself in a good story? By the end, you don't even remember your own name because the author's words have immersed you in that world, ripping you away from your own perspective and painting another all around you. This is the intention with manifestational writing. Play with it. Be passionate. Be silly. Lose yourself in the fun of it all. Powerful joyous emotion is a sign that our "Kundalini," or base spiritual energy, is being stimulated and rising within. The more joy and belief you pour into these writings, the swifter and more fluid the manifestation will arrive.

Change is a process, but with a little effort, through prayer, meditation and writing, you can birth something in the nonphysical, then pull it towards you in the physical, fanning your emotional flames as you go. Again, the words themselves are not pertinent. Sometimes you don't know the best course of action. Sometimes you think one reality will bring you great joy, but in truth this is just a desire of the ego, and if manifested, would not bring you the satisfaction you imagine it would. Our Higher Selves do not need directions. We are using the journals for ourselves, not to tell Spirit what we want, but to find that emotional place inside us to sustain the joyous emotion that matches the vibration of that which we seek. So write, write and write some more. Then let it all go. Allow having the dream to be enough for the moment. Keep your sights on your destiny. Allow yourself to get lost in the present because appreciating the now is the swiftest way to allow the future you have asked for to integrate itself into your experience.

A lot of people learn of the law of attraction, try to "use" or "harness" it, don't have immediate results, and then give up claiming "it doesn't work." When I was young, if my mother was helping me with a project and I got discouraged, she would immediately stop, sit down and wait. She would say "Okay, well if you decide you can't do it there is nothing in my power I can do to change that, because you are too powerful. I cannot change your current, but I'll be here when you remember what you can do." In my adolescence I did not find this helpful, only now do I understand the wisdom my mother was giving me. Learning to consciously manipulate your reality takes time and dedication. It might happen differently than you imagined, some things may never materialize. Take the things that don't manifest as you intended as a sign that Spirit has something else planned or perhaps that road was not as prosperous as you originally conceived.

Programming your matrix doesn't stop at journal entries. Life is a meditation, if you allow it to be. In a day there are a thousand things to react to, to give your power and your joy away. Attempt to pull your focus back to zero point consciousness, back to a perspective of peace and fluidity. Wake up each morning intending to push your focus into the place of love that will be most beneficial for your life experience. It isn't easy at first, especially when we are used to being immersed in static, but as you transmute and release the various aspects of your ego, and make way for your light to integrate once again, it will become easier. First you intend it, create it, birth it, fan the flames in the non-physical, then go out into the world and take steps towards your goal (even if they are small steps at first)! Don't force it, wait for the inspiration catalyzed by your intentions. Choice and action are as much a part of creating your reality as emotion and thought. Spirit will bring you the opportunities, then you must walk the path.

MORE WAYS TO PROGRAM YOUR MATRIX:

Gratitude Lists: Feed and sustain your abundant vibrations with appreciation. Take some time each day to either mentally note, or write down all of the gifts you are given on a daily basis. Nothing is too small to be on a gratitude list, and the more you do it, the more the good in your life grows and multiplies.

Make a vision board: You can do this digitally or on paper, find pictures that represent what you are trying to manifest and arrange them together in a collage. Place it somewhere you will see it often, like up on your wall, or as your computer display screen.

Labels: I have a dear friend who turned me onto labeling my water bottles with intention to charge the water with positive vibrations, now I am labeling everything. Scatter notes of intention all around where you are living or working to inspire and focus your energy throughout the day.

Training your brain with binaural beats: Binaural beats can assist you in training your brainwaves into higher states of consciousness that will make your mind more malleable and therefore able to focus on what you are desiring to bring into manifestation. You can find a multitude of free binaural beat meditations on youtube.

Arts: Are you an artist? Do you make music? If so, paint a picture of what you want, or write a song that takes you to the emotional place of its manifestation. This is very powerful because you are activating your second chakra and allowing your creative energies to flow through you which can greatly accelerate your results.

VISUALIZATIONS

These next few pages are a collection of visualizations that you can use in your meditations to communicate and work with the unseen realms. Use them as you are inspired to do so and don't be afraid to build upon them and make them your own. The ability to visualize varies from person to person, but intention is the most important aspect of the practice. All of us have the ability to hone these skills. You don't need to see every detail. Do your best, and when the ego is trying to interrupt, just let the thoughts pass through you and move your mind back to the task at hand.

Using visualizations in your meditative practice can yield incredibly powerful results. Anything that is manifest in the physical world began first in the non-physical. Visualizations give you an interface to communicate and create consciously with your Higher Self, guides and the unseen dimensions of your multi-verse. Explore your energy and ask questions when you are communicating with them. Be direct, concise and clear. Let the answers come as they do, whether through insight, image, feeling or symbols. Be patient with yourself. Energy healing isn't always obvious in the moment, but you can be sure with dedicated practice, you will create miraculous results.

Each meditation is an opportunity to explore and convene with the unseen realms. If you add these visualizations to your "psychic dictionary" you can use them to translate and work in those dimensions. Spirit will respond and the more you persevere on your spiritual path the easier it will be to see, hear and discern their guidance.

THE VIOLET FLAME

The Violet Flame is a sacred violet fire that can be summoned for cleansing, purification and transformation. Call upon its power to transmute your being on a cellular level. See it engulf you in your meditations burning away all of your dense emotions, beliefs and earthly attachments. This is a universally positive energy and is also a powerful aid when you want to ground light into Mother Earth. Simply see violet fire burning easily around your point of focus whether it be yourself, or the whole world. Call upon Ascended Master St. Germaine, the keeper of the Violet Flame to cleanse and rejuvenate your spirit from any and all earthly density. This flame is coveted in Elemental realms because of its potent vibration which can affect nature and the earth in a profound way. So next time you are looking at a polluted, ignored or exhausted part of Mother Earth, send some Violet Flame that way. She will be grateful for the light and you are assisting in raising the vibration of the space so it can manifest healing for itself.

GROUNDING

In order to achieve all the dreams we wish to manifest into our realities, we must be grounded and connected to Mother Earth. If we are not grounded we may have difficulty staying focused, caring for the physical body and environment, creating enough cash flow to feel safe and provided for in your experience and so on. Here are two grounding meditations to root your energy into the earth, so you can connect to her love, care and abundance. These visualizations are best done outside on the dirt or grass, but are still effective when indoors.

Grounding Cord:

This is for everyday use. I begin each meditation by turning my root chakra into a long red tube and then watching it root into the core of the earth. You can repeat this throughout the day if you start feeling ungrounded. This will bring your energy back into the body and assist you in focusing and feeling safe in your daily life.

Becoming A Tree:

This one is more appropriate when you are in need Mother Earth's strength and power to stand tall. It can be incredibly powerful to absorb and embrace her medicinal magic in this way Imagine yourself in a meadow, feeling the soft grass beneath your feet, the sun and wind across your face, fall into yourself, breathing deeply and with your exhale push your energy down towards the earth. See the energy you are pushing into the ground as bright strands of red light and intend for them to reach deeply into the core of the earth. Feel that red light traveling back up through the roots into your feet, up your legs, passed your chest and face covering your whole being with this warm red liquid light. After you are completely covered, feel this energy hardening around you growing and changing, see it transforming you into a great big tree. Survey what kind of tree you changed into and perhaps look into the symbolism afterwards. Feel your arms as long strong branches reaching towards the universe receiving and grounding divine light. Sit here as long as you like absorbing the medicine.

Going Underground:

Last but not least, this can be used for someone with high anxiety or stress levels. Feel your energy go deep underground, and bury itself within the earth. Far enough that you feel completely enveloped in her warmth. Letting go of all influences and fears you are carrying on the surface and allowing the dirt to warm and nurture you. Then feel green liquid light coming from all directions within you from the earth, allow it to calm your spirit, and fill you with unconditionally loving energy. Often when I use this I will hear the earth soothing me, assuring that I belong here, and that all will be well. This is particularly good for someone in the midst of an anxiety or panic attack. When you become a tree, you are summoning the strength to stand tall, and be seen. Going underground assists with deep healing, and protection from external energetic static.

AN EXCERPT ON THE ELEMENTS:

The elements make up all forms of matter in existence, at least all that we are aware of. You can call upon the elements and use them in your alchemical pursuits. My recommendation is to understand that each element has a different purpose and personality, and from that knowing getting to know each one so you can use them in a way that is aligned with your highest good. Early alchemists focused heavily on understanding the spiritual implications of the elemental forces which make up our world. Call upon the elements in your meditations, spend time with each one using the invocations below, or your own. Ask your Higher Self to guide you in learning about the elements safely and to show you which ones will benefit you most as you walk along your healing path. When speaking or thinking the invocation, visualize a representation of that element's energy traveling through your cells and energetic bodies.

Earth: Earth will ground you and absorb heaviness from your energy bodies. It is the element that governs your foundation and physical existence. It can assist you with the practical and physical responsibilities in your life as well as fill you with feelings of warmth, love, and security. Associated Chakra: Root

Invocation: *I invoke the power of the Earth element, and allow it to ground and balance my energetic bodies. I ask to be stable, grounded, and responsible for my physical existence. I allow it to birth all vibrational seeds that I have planted, that are in line with my highest good, and that it absorbs any density I am ready to let go of in the now*

Water: Water is about depth, birth, dreams, psychic awareness, and intuition. Call upon water to cool your emotional space, (especially if you have been overdoing it with fire). While fire burns away density, water cleanses and absorbs it. Water hides much under the surface and thus it is the gateway to our subconscious. It is feminine by nature and can cleanse away dense energy. Associated Chakra: Sacral

Invocation: *I invoke the power of the Water element, allowing it to purify my psychic and intuitive streams of consciousness. I allow it to cool and cleanse my energetic bodies on a cellular level, and ask that all that is hidden in my emotional subconscious is safely brought to the surface for purification and awareness.*

Air: Air is about freedom, and weightlessness. Call upon the element of air to lighten your energy and assist you in navigating the realms of thought and imagination. Air is spiritual sustenance which is why the breath is so sacred and important. Air is deeply connected to fire in that without oxygen, our inner flame becomes extinguished, that teaches us that if our energy is very heavy and unable to breathe freely, our inner spark begins to dwindle. Associated Chakra: Heart.

Invocation: *I invoke the power of the Air element to elevate me above my earthly worries and assist with me traversing through the realms of thought and imagination. I ask to be completely sustained spiritually, and to inundate myself with the sacred nature of my breath. Lighten my emotional load and assist me in flying above the density which manifests in my life experience.*

Fire: Call upon fire to ignite powerful, passionate, emotion within you and to burn away anything you no longer wish to carry on an energetic level. Beware not to overuse it as too much fire can result in angry mood swings, or lashing out in ways we wish we hadn't. Fire motivates and transmutes, but if used too often it will burn. Fire is wild in itself, it needs earth to ground it, air to give it life, and water to put it out, so before calling upon the fire element make sure you are grounded, and in balance. Associated Chakra: Solar Plexus.

Invocation: *I invoke the power of the Fire element, to motivate me in passionately following my inspiration, and to have all the strength necessary to achieve my highest dreams and aspirations. I ask that is burns away all resistance or density that I am ready to let go of in the now, and transmutes all cold or deadened parts of my spirit.*

Spirit: Spirit is the fifth element, and the vibrational glue which holds all the elements in their place. It is divine light, the energy of creation itself that connects each and every strand of matter in existence. It is the collective divine consciousness, which is at the base of all that is in this Universe. Associated Chakras: Throat, Third Eye, Crown.

Invocation: *I invoke the element of Spirit to travel through me, awakening my spiritual knowledge, memories, and abilities. I allow my divinity to be seen and expressed within myself and let go of any spiritual density which is keeping me from embracing my light.*

WORKING WITH YOUR CHAKRAS:

To begin working with your chakras in meditation, spin each one from root to crown, seeing them one after the other begin widening and spinning clock-wise. Open them as wide as feels comfortable and natural. When you exercise the physical body you create movement to stimulate it, this is what we are doing when we are opening and spinning our chakra system. This is the second step of all of my meditations right after letting down my grounding cord because it sets an intention telling my energy body that I am ready to work with and explore it, opening my chakra system to the flow of cosmic energies available from the realms of Spirit. When you have made it to the crown chakra, you are ready to begin seeing the state of your energy body.

Begin to create a dialogue with your Higher Self. Ask them to show you your chakra system and survey its current state. How do your chakras appear to you? How do they feel? Go through each chakra, root to crown, seeing if they are balanced, overactive, under-active or shut down. Your chakras work as a system, you want them all to be balanced and in sync. If you are not able to see them in your mind's eye, just relax and allow the insights to come as they do. The more meditation you integrate into your experience the easier it will be for Spirit to get through the various veils of resistance. Refrain from putting pressure on yourself and keep coming back to seeing and reviewing the state of your chakra system as it progresses and your sight clears. If you are going through your chakra system and it seems like it requires extensive repair then perhaps seek out a healer with more experience in the unseen realms to guide you through any chakra trauma or repressed pain that seems overwhelming.

After you have gone through mentally noting (or writing down) the surface view of your chakras, it's time to create a dialogue and begin communicating with them. One way to communicate with your chakra system is by seeing your chakras as a house. Each room representing a different chakra. Go through this house and ask yourself how it feels inside. What is the foundation like? Does it require repairs? Spend time in your chakra house seeing which rooms need upkeep, and fix what you see that requires attention. Go back when you are inspired and continue working, even redecorating or adding things that feel appropriate. It may sound silly, but it can have profound effects in your life by dedicating some TLC to your chakra house.

Another path of communication with your chakras is by seeing or imagining them personified. See each chakra as a light being in front of you and ask them questions. It helps to write these down as it can be difficult to recall all the answers when you leave the trance state. Let them tell you if they require healing, attention or further exploration. Send them light and learn to listen to your energy body for it will tell you what it requires.

Ask your Higher Self and guides to balance and cleanse your chakras of any densities which are keeping you from your highest good. Get to know your energy body and learn what it needs so you can give it to yourself. Continue to revisit and nurture your chakra system just as you do the physical body, and eagerly anticipate the magic to start reflecting in your physical world.

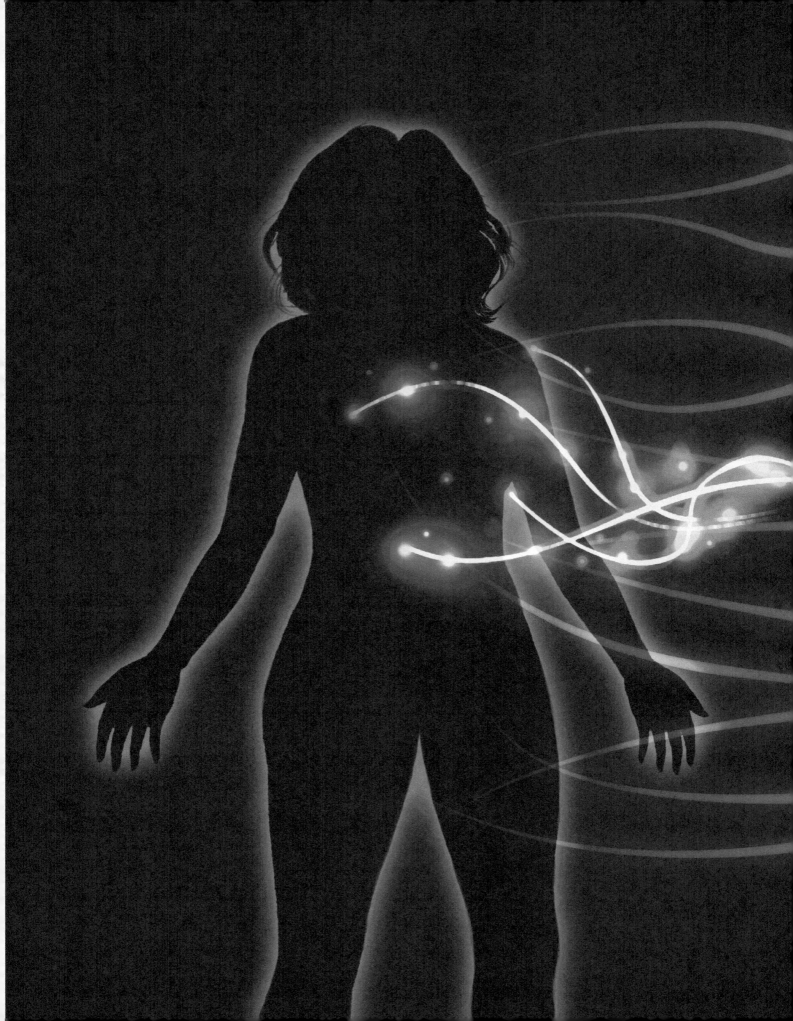

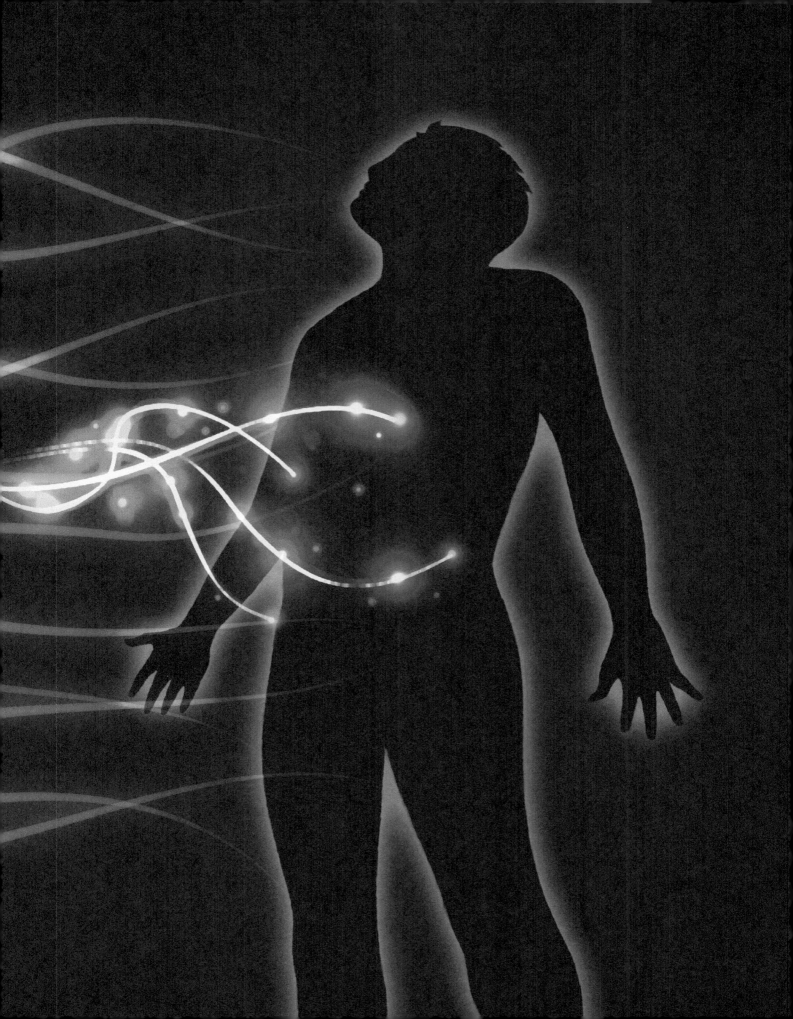

ENERGY CORDS

Anytime you attach emotion to something or someone an energetic cord is born. We all have energy cords connecting us to people, events in our lives, and situations, clearing away your negative corded attachments will free up your energy so you can use it constructively instead of siphoning it away to external stimuli. I won't be going into finding specific cords yourself because this is an introductory text and that is a more advanced practice that requires a good deal of explanation and instruction, but asking your Higher Self to remove excess cords which are no longer serving your highest good is the first step in healing your energetic cording. If you want to get more specific or already know that you have deep cords with a certain person or trauma and wish to let them go, then again, ask your Higher Self to lead you to a healer or teacher with more experience in the unseen realms to hold space and guide you through any large cords that may be siphoning away your energy and power.

General Cord Pulling Invocation:

I ask my Higher Self to pull all energetic cords of density that are corded to me which I am ready to release and let go of now. I ask that light is sent to whatever I am severing my connection to, and that all empty parts of me where cords are released are refilled with light as well. If deeper processing need occur, I ask to be led to a healer who can guide me through deep cords and hold space for my healing release.

By my own free will, in gratitude, and so it is.

THE AKASHIC RECORDS

The Akashic Library is a nonphysical location which houses all of the information from our human incarnations. Travel there in meditation to learn about yourself and your life purpose. Visualize a large elevator with pearly white doors, step within and with your intention shoot yourself upwards and as the doors open once again you are greeted by grand steps to an immaculate floating library. When you arrive on the steps of this magnificent library in the sky, feel the cold stone walking towards the door, and see a robed guide waiting for you at the entrance. Think of this as your Akashic librarian, and ask them to lead you to whatever knowledge you are seeking. If you do not have a direct question, simply ask why you have been called there, and what wisdom can be imparted from the records during your visit. Then let them lead you inside to a book of their choosing, open the book, and allow whatever visions or information which are inspired to come through. This is a good place to go if you have questions about past or parallel lifetimes. Keep a notebook close by!

BURNING CONTRACTS:

Your Higher Self made contracts for your life before this incarnation and continues to do so from the other side. They are agreements about what you will accomplish and learn during this incarnation. Examples include: who your family will be, who you will get to meet and know during your life, what the dynamic will be in all of your relationships, where you will grow up, what your spiritual purpose is, contracts between you and you Spirit guides, emotional contracts, karmic agreements, traumas and illnesses you may experience and more. Some contracts are of a beneficial nature, but negative contracts that have been made could be hindering your experience. Ask your guides to show you any negative or dense contracts that have been born in this or any other dimension in which you have been manifest. Once you have read and understand the contracts and have decided you want to let go of the agreement, see it burst into flames (I often use violet) and disintegrate the contract from your energetic blueprint.

SHADOW PURGE

This is a way to release dense energy safely and easily. In the event that a negative emotion or energy surfaces while you are in meditation or that was catalyzed by the outside world and you want to release it, first identify what the emotion is. When you feel clear on its identity and are ready to let it go, start to see it as dark smoke or liquid all around you. Then, begin to feel and see it bunching together and centering before your eyes. Pull your breath deeply into the pit of your stomach and on your next exhale fiercely push the dark energy into the earth with your breath to be planted as newborn energy. Sometimes it feels like you need to push it out a few times, but it can be quite the cathartic release. When you are finished, cleanse the earth where the energy was sent with the Violet Flame to thoroughly transmute the density and thank Mother Earth for holding space for your healing. Then, after checking your grounding cord to make sure it is intact, ask your Higher Self to fill you with light, replenishing all of the density you just released.

BUTTERFLIES

Have you ever seen the metamorphosis of a caterpillar? If not I have your next youtube suggestion. The caterpillar essentially dies and a new being, the butterfly, is born from what the caterpillar began. Butterfly medicine is about total rebirth and transformation. See yourself surrounded in a swarm of butterflies to call upon a personal metamorphosis. Feel their paper thin wings flapping all around you and allow them to eat away any parts of yourself that you are ready to let go of, so you are able to grow into the next version of yourself. Send gratitude to the butterflies for contributing to your healing and allow them to take any heaviness away from your energetic field. Send them to places which you feel require energetic clean up or transformation.

ELEPHANT BATH

Call to the Elephants when you are in need of stability and strength. Visualize yourself in a watering hole surrounded by large Elephants. Ask them to cleanse your energy and give you the strength you need to tackle whatever challenge is in front of you at that time. Lie in the middle of the watering hole and wait as they begin to dance. Feel their feet moving in unison and see your stress or fear as black water coming out from your feet into the watering hole. Elephants care deeply for all things and can teach us how to stay in our power in a gentle and loving way. This visualization came to me during a strenuous part of my life, I felt the Elephants dancing around me and my stress leaving my body, transmuting itself in their watering hole. I felt comforted by their presence and allowed the dance they were doing to put me deep in trance. When I awoke I felt ready to deal with my life and the challenges I was facing. They are ancient wise spirits and will cleanse all who call to them.

MORE ANIMAL SYMBOLISM:

Butterflies and Elephants are two of the creatures I visit the most often in meditation, but all animals and insects carry a unique spiritual medicine with them that you can tap into and learn from. Below are a few more of my go-tos that you can incorporate into your visualizations, and some of the medicinal symbolism they carry.

Lion: They will assist in standing in your individuality, spiritual power and natural strength.

Snake: The bringer of hidden knowledge and transformation. They can assist you in shedding skins of past selves.

Wolf: Connect and attune to your natural instincts and assist in sharpening your mental powers.

Horse: Their medicine helps with overcoming obstacles on your path, and expressing yourself freely with assertion.

Owl: Uncover what is hidden, strengthen your intuition, and intend to seek wisdom in all regards. They symbolize change, death and rebirth.

Whale: Ancient sacred beings who have been revered throughout history as wise old teachers. They can assist with all forms of communication, and will guide you through ancestral journeying.

Spider: They weave and thus create with ease, spiders can assist you in manifesting and creating what you desire patiently, as well as navigating through your shadow selves.

Hawk: Spirit messengers pay attention when these birds cross your path, they help you clear your vision, strengthen your intuition, and allow divine messages to become manifest.

CAULDRONS

Cauldrons have been used in magical practice for centuries. In many belief systems, the cauldron is associated with the Goddess as it is connected to the ideas of birth and the womb. Use cauldrons in your visualizations to birth new creations into your reality, connect with your feminine energy, or even as a portal to see into other worlds. Place inside a symbol of whatever you are trying to see or affect, then see the flames growing and the steam of your intention rising into the ethers. Feel light flowing out of your hands into the cauldron and being sent into the object of your attention, raising its vibration and bringing it closer to you. Then stare into the surface of the water and see what messages Spirit has for you. When you are finished send gratitude to the cauldron for acting as a womb for whatever you are desiring to bring into manifestation or clarity.

ENERGY BUBBLES

Energy bubbles can be used for different healing purposes in your meditation and daily life. Each color has a specific healing vibration and effect, that I have briefly summarized below. When you are familiar with the meanings you can use them upon inspiration from your guides within. Listen to your body and spirit to feel what color bubble would be most beneficial in the moment.

Red Bubble: Red is connected with earth energy and brings the heat. It can be used to burn away deep core childhood trauma, rebuild emotional strength, clear away sickness and physical dis-ease, bring passion back into your experience and ground your spirit in the physical body. It can bring life and warmth to any cold or "dead" parts of your mind, body or spirit.

Orange Bubble: Accelerating manifestation, healing sexual trauma, increasing sexual energy, encouraging creativity and strengthening the physical body.

Yellow Bubble: Increasing self esteem, strengthening willpower, creating mental and emotional clarity, increasing joyous emotion or burning away resistance to effort and success.

Green Bubble: Filling yourself with heart centered energy, good for healing on all levels physical, spiritual, and emotional, attracting prosperity, soothing anxiety, combating depression.

Blue Bubble: Facilitating clear and authentic communication, alleviating hyper self-critical thoughts, calming or cooling the mind, body, and spirit, attracting inner peace.

Indigo Bubble: Activating psychic and intuitive gifts, calming the spirit, facilitating a trance state, promoting feelings of freedom and heightening intuition.

Violet Bubble: Spiritual transmutation or transformation, aligning you with your highest spiritual intention, becoming closer to the divine energies.

Pink Bubble: Unconditional love energy, heart healing, facilitating comfort, creating compassion and supporting habits of self care.

White Bubble: Divine protection from toxic energies or psychic attack, purifying or healing the mind, body, and spirit, invoking angelic presence, burning away painful emotions or energies.

Rainbow Bubble: Balancing your whole chakra system, deep cleansing of your auric fields and energy bodies, soothing heartache, invoking abundance, improving mental clarity.

AFFIRMATIONS

Words carry great power. Everything you think and speak are affirmations in some way or another, weaving threads to the tapestry that is your manifested reality. Every sentence is a spell cast. Speak with care and intention, to yourself and others. Often our inner voice is still the recycled voice of an abusive childhood or wounded ego. Do not own that voice as your own. Combat the whispers of the ego by feeding your soul with positive affirmations and intentions. Affirmations strengthen your vibration, quicken manifestation and can be used all throughout the day. These are some of the affirmations I have written for myself and gladly pass on, but nothing is more powerful than tapping into your own creative stream and finding the ones that come from your heart. Repeat them as often as you are guided to do so.

General Cleansing Affirmation:

I cleanse my mind, body and spirit of any and all density that may have attached itself or been grown from within throughout my journey here. I burn away all foreign, vampiric or toxic energies that I may have come across in this timeline and all other dimensions where my spirit has been manifest, past, present or future. I allow the light of my Higher Self to cleanse, clear and invigorate me. I give myself permission to cleanse and purge my energetic streams, asking to be supported and held by Spirit throughout the remainder of the cleansing process. I am cleansed. I am whole. I am a vessel for the divine energy and allow this cleansing and reinvigoration to be received. By my own free will, in gratitude, and so it is.

Ego Release: —When you have discovered an aspect of your ego which you would like to bring into awareness or eventual release. Affirming the awareness of the aspect will start the process of circulating that quality out of the small self for transmutation— *I allow the awareness of (insert shadow aspect/emotion here) to come up for processing and release. I allow the root of this issue to come to the surface sending light, illumination, realization and healing to this pocket of shadow I have discovered. I forgive this aspect of my ego, and acknowledge its purpose in my growth and evolution as a soul. I take responsibility for and release said emotion/aspect of yourself, roots and all, back into Mother Earth to be transmuted and birthed anew as she replenishes and reinvigorates my energy. I understand that we all have shadow to clear from this journey and I am appreciative that this aspect was discovered so that I may now let it go. By my own free will, in gratitude, and so it is.*

New Moon Cleansing:

On this eve of the new moon I plant my seeds of intention deep into the earth to be circulated and manifested during this lunar cycle, or in perfect divine timing. I surrender my resistance to the manifestation of my greatest good to Mother Earth and allow the Goddess energy to birth and nurture my seeds. In this moment I am reborn, walking into this cycle with joyous anticipation to the miracles waiting just beyond the horizon. I am cleansed, protected, and surrounded in the presence of my Higher Self and unseen friends. They will provide support and care throughout this lunar cycle. I await and appreciate All That Is and all that is to come. By my own free will, in gratitude, and so it is.

Full Moon Cleansing:

On this eve of the full moon, I allow my energy to be cleansed and reinvigorated. I allow my emotions to be as full and vivid as they are, and surrender all resistance to this energetic purge. I allow my intentions to manifest the seeds which I have planted, through the release of any density allowed by the power yielded during the full moon. I align myself with the currents of this lunar cycle and am surrounded in divine support, guidance and unconditional love. By my own free will, in gratitude, and so it is.

Health:

I am feeling stronger in each moment. My body is healthy now. My body regenerates itself on all levels and is doing so every moment of every day. I make healthy lifestyle choices and see results quickly when I intend to improve my physical well being. I love my cells. My cells radiate with love and stimulation. I feel invigorated and alive. I spread love and appreciation to each and every one of my cells. My body speaks to me and tells me what's wrong, I can intuitively feel what would bring it the most relief. Thank you for leading me to any and all healers, physicians or medicinal treatments that would be most beneficial for my mind, body, spirit, connection. My body is watched over by my Higher Self and I release all attachments to sickness and dis-ease now. I allow any energetic density in regards to my physical body to arise for processing then release, and affirm I am guided through that process by my team of healing guides who surround me always. By my own free will, in gratitude, and so it is.

Abundance:

I am abundant now in all areas of my experience. All that I require comes to me with great ease. I trust that spirit will always provide for me, and allow the manifestation of their support to fluidly fall into my experience. I am abundant in air, water, food and shelter.

I am abundant in love and the whispering fire of Spirit. My life reflects miraculous abundance in all of its aspects. All that I ask for is given to me, exactly as it should be. I trust in divine timing and appreciate all abundance I am blessed with, in my reality. By my own free will, in gratitude, and so it is.

Changing Money Perception/Surrender Poverty Vows:

I surrender all attachments or vows of poverty in this timeline and all others where my energetic expression is manifest. I surrender any demonizing perceptions of monetary or economic abundance. I love money. I love the way it feels in my hands, I love the smell of money, I love having all the money I need to comfortably live and enjoy my experience. Money is energy. Money comes to me effortlessly with ease and grace. I love seeing the creative ways that Spirit will orchestrate the arrival of my financial abundance. By my own free will, in gratitude, and so it is.

Grounding Abundance Affirmation:

I ground and root myself deep into Mother Earth now, allowing her to pull me into her infinite stream of abundant unconditional love and support, providing all that I desire and sustaining the love, comfort and strength radiating from her womb to my soul. I can feel her telling me I am worthy of this abundance now. I feel her whispering of new and brighter horizons, as she holds my hand, assuring me I am never alone. I am worthy of this abundance now and allow it to manifest with graceful ease. Each day I root into Mother Earth, allowing her light and abundance to bloom plentifully throughout my life experience. By my own free will, in gratitude, and so it is.

Joy Affirmation:

My life is full of joy. Each day brings a cornucopia of possibilities which I can choose to immerse myself in. I cherish each moment I spend smiling, as I understand that each is a gift and should be coveted as such. I choose joy now, and release any and all energetic density that sits in my present moment keeping me from feeling my true power. My joy is not dependent on external validation, but sustained by my connection with my inner and true self. My life is joyful even through the frustration and density. I give myself permission to slow down and smell the roses. I give my permission to keep my joy rather than giving it away to the various influences of my day. I appreciate all moments that take me away from joy so when I arrive there again I can appreciate it even more. By my own free will, in gratitude, and so it is.

Adventure:

I surrender and release any and all beliefs that keep me imprisoned in limitation, or the mundane. I allow Spirit to flow vividly through my experience illuminating the fire in my heart and the desire of my soul. I seek to experience and make this intention known to this universe and my unseen friends. I replace my fear with faith, and release all density that keeps me frozen in a repetitive or monotonous situation. I allow my divine soul mission to be fully and consciously realized and surrender all resistance to the achievement of abundance, success and adventure. I forgive my fear and take my power back from it now. I trust that Spirit will guide this adventure and open me up to the manifested path of possibilities which will lead to my greatest and most prized salvation. By my own free will, in gratitude, and so it is.

Permission Affirmation:

I give myself permission to unravel. I give myself permission to let go and breathe deep. I give myself permission not to have it all together, and not to have it all figured out. I give myself permission to be still, and true to myself. I give myself permission to grow, change, evolve and move. I give myself permission to learn lessons. I give chaos permission. I give Spirit permission to lead me in fresh and new directions. I surrender my control, and allow the cosmic flow of creation to lead me towards my most beneficial trajectory. Every step that I have taken up to this point has been okay. I surrender regret, and allow the wisdom of all of my lessons to integrate and ground within me. I give myself permission to be silly and to make mistakes. I give myself permission to not know all the answers. This experience is exploratory; I surrender all pressures. I respect the chaotic and dualistic nature of creation and allow the waves to manifest and be as they will. I give myself permission to be who I am and not put other's needs above my own. I give myself permission to love slowly, to stop and nurture stillness, to watch the birds as they soar through the skies. I give myself permission to be vulnerable and poetic, passionate and ignited. I give myself permission to be wild, to be crazy, to have no filters or masks. Today I am me. All is well. I give myself permission to be free and to embrace each and every moment of this experience with ecstatic appreciation. All is well. All is changing. I'm okay. Life is good. By my own free will, in gratitude, and so it is.

Grief/Self Care:

It's okay that it hurts right now. I surrender fighting against my pain and understand that this is a part of my growth. In my surrendering of the fight, I allow the pain to wash through me instead of attempting to escape it. I honor my grief. I honor my emotional body and my sensitive heart space, which is blessed to feel and experience life. I give myself the space I require to compassionately and lovingly lead myself through this brief tunnel of darkness. I know there is light on the other side. I know that this will pass and soon my clarity and strength will rejuvenate, and I will be greater than I was before. Pain is temporary. Life is a gift. I will take this darkness and alchemize it into something new, and while I allow myself to rest and grieve for the moment, I know that I am a Phoenix and soon this ash will turn to flame, birthing me anew, and igniting my spark once again. It's okay to be sad. It's okay to not understand or have it all figured out. Now I will rest. I will allow myself all I require to heal and grow stronger and wiser from these lessons. I am grateful for my ability to be hurt, for it indicates my ability to feel, to connect and to love. I'm going to do whatever I have to do for myself because I am worthy of this self care, and my emotional wellbeing is important and sacred. I call upon the Divine Mother now and allow her to wrap her arms around me, cradling *me, providing for me and guiding me into the light where I may rest and recover. By my own free will, in gratitude, and so it is.*

"I AM"

When you say "I AM" what you are really saying is "I am all things. I am Source energy. I am all that is. I am Goddess/God, I am Spirit." You are remembering your divine identity and affirming it to the world.

IN CONCLUSION

The future is in our hands. May we embrace our divinity and remember the power we have to influence the world around us. Distraction abounds, the shadow powers which have held its grip on this realm are flooding our realities with static to keep us from the awakening that is being born here, but they shall not succeed. They do not have the power to stand up against the masters that are here at this time or to bring down this cycle which is transforming our collective with each passing second. Their time is up and a time of great light will arise in its wake. Go inward and empower yourself with your gifts. Remember who you are and claim your right to a joyous and loving experience. Befriend the army that surrounds you and connect with the totality of your power, ground it in your life and use it to contribute to the new world we are creating.

Before we finish the race, we are tested on all that we have learned. This time of global chaos and confusion is a part of that testing, which is why you can see so many parallels from the past revealing themselves to us. The planets and the stars are all working together to chisel us into the best versions of ourselves that we can be. This process can feel daunting at times, but when you feel lost look upward. Seek the light and it will find you. Love as often as you can, forgive easily and let go of anything that keeps you tethered in density. When you fall down, get back up. Stay strong and take nothing for granted. Trust that we are being guided and that goodness will prevail. Appreciate the gift of life and embrace all the opportunities Spirit gives you to grow. Stand out. Shine your light. Live by the glowing clarity of your awakened example. You are miraculous. You are a soul who has embarked on a physical journey and you have chosen a world full of many forms of activity to explore and experience. You are brave and you can do anything. Ignore the voices in your head telling you otherwise and dedicate yourself to achieving all of your dreams.

Your dreams are a gift. Your inspirations are from the highest light of All That Is, and they seek you as they whisper into your heart. You are not alone, and you are not small. Don't let the world make you feel that way. You have greatness within you, and it will lead you where you are meant to go.

Meet the Author!

My journey communicating with Spirit began early. I can remember drawing a door on the wall of my parents' home at three years old, walking through, and finding myself in a musky grotto with a radiant Goddess waiting for me at the end of an ice cream cone bridge. That may sound silly but it is one of my earliest memories voyaging within the unseen

realms. In my adolescence, I ran away from my abilities, quieting the wounds of childhood trauma with substance abuse. Through dedication to my spiritual evolution, I fought my way out of that world and was led by Spirit from darkness into light. Today, I work with people to assist in processing their various soul traumas, helping them to remember their innate divine power, and giving them tools to connect with their Spirit guides and Higher Self. I am certified in Clairvoyant Intuitive Studies, Vibrational Healing, and Trance Vocal Channeling, a graduate of the Multidimensional Healing Program from the school "Sacred Connections" and recognized by the International Assembly of Spiritual Healers and Earth Steward Congregations as an Ordained Minister, Certified Spiritual Healer, and Diplomat of Earth Stewardship.

CPSIA information can be obtained
at www.ICGtesting.com
Printed in the USA
BVOW05s0609291017
498905BV00022B/331/P

9 780999 215616